P9-DTE-142

Gambling on Granola

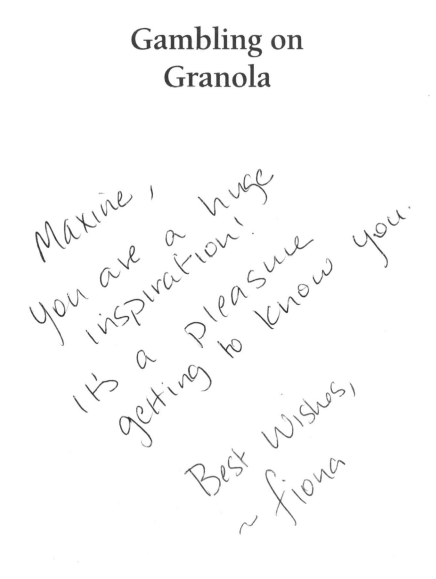

Maxine,
you are a huge
inspiration!
It's a pleasure
getting to know you.

Best wishes,
~ fiona

Gambling on Granola

Unexpected Gifts on the Path of Entrepreneurship

Fiona Maria Simon

Terra Nova Books
SANTA FE, NEW MEXICO

Some names have been changed to protect the privacy of those depicted.

Library of Congress Control Number 2017952746

Distributed by SCB Distributors, (800) 729-6423

Terra Nova Books

Gambling on Granola. Copyright © 2018 by Fiona Simon
All rights reserved
Printed in the United States of America

No part of this book may be used or reproduced in any manner whatsoever without written permission except in the case of brief quotations embedded in critical articles and reviews. Send inquiries to Terra Nova Books, 33 Alondra Road, Santa Fe, New Mexico 87508.

Published by Terra Nova Books, Santa Fe, New Mexico.
www.TerraNovaBooks.com

ISBN 978-1-938288-92-0

This book is dedicated to my daughter, Natalie, for whom I started my granola company, and to my grandmother, MM, who was the first to say I would become a writer.

It is also dedicated to the many colorful characters I've written about. Not only did you shape my world for well over a decade but you also shaped this story.

~Contents~

~1~
LIVES DIVIDED

"Follow your spirit, without hesitation."
—Anonymous
(Quote on caddies of Cranberry Orange Granola Bars)

"The shadow never enters a room without a gift in its hands." A friend once shared this quote with me, and I have always found it true. In the spring of 2000, a particularly gloomy shadow entered my life. Its presence announced a division of lives and time and space, and departure from a comfortable existence that allowed much freedom and decision-making. My world turned upside down from one day to the next, and I turned topsy-turvy along with it.

The request for a divorce came without warning. My husband and I got along well, were great friends, and shared completely the joys of parenthood and the love of our daughter, Natalie, who was about to turn three. But his resolve was set; the separation of lives began. We sold the house, moved into smaller places, and I quickly found work as communications director of the Boulder, Colorado, Chamber of Commerce. I had been a writer for most of my career, and the position seemed a good fit for my background. With shared custody—a continuing cycle of five days with me, two with her dad, two with me, and five with her dad—and both parents at work full time, Natalie also transitioned. We placed her in a delightful Montessori preschool, which soon felt like family. Precocious, sociable, happy, and always eager to learn and explore, Natalie immediately felt at home in her new school.

I was largely relieved that my daughter loved her school and was well taken care of. I also enjoyed my days. Evenings and weekends, however, were a different story. Being alone in the house with no family to share it was almost unbearable. Weekends were long and lonely. In short order, I became depressed and despondent. I yearned to change my life so that I could see my daughter more often and gather together as a family. No aspect of my existence—mental, emotional, physical, or spiritual—was functioning in a healthy manner. I was suddenly a single mom, and my life was dictated by my work schedule. From one day to the next, I transitioned from a full-time mother to a full-time employee. I had gone from sharing my days with Natalie to sharing my days with coworkers. Along with that severe change, custody was split evenly, which meant I could be with Natalie only half the time. Having limited access to my daughter was the most painful aspect of the divorce, and it hit me harder than I could have imagined. The waves of depression were fierce, and they manifested themselves physically, plunging me to dark depths of fatigue, insomnia, and inability to focus.

Some nights—once a week or so—I could sense the "glob" coming in. The front door appeared to open on its own, and a big, heavy mass of black goop entered the room and slowly made its way toward me. I remained paralyzed, watching it approach, knowing I had to surrender. It entered my body, feeling as if some great, heavy force was slowly passing through, taking over, consuming me physically and emotionally. My breaths became short as I sat there, waiting to discover what might happen next.

Then the force was suddenly gone, as if it had had its way with me and no longer felt the need to stay. The episodes lasted only a few minutes, but they terrified me. They also became more frequent, every few days or so. There were nights when I'd sit at the dining room table, sipping a glass of wine or smoking a little pot to soothe my nerves, waiting for the glob. "Come on in," I'd yell into the room, "just get it over with." I never knew when to expect that ugly glob. I only knew I wanted it out of my life.

There was just one solution: make permanent, tangible changes that would allow me to cope with this new way of life. I decided to focus on one thing: change my situation into something positive.

The soul searching began. Each day at lunchtime, I pounded the pavement, contemplating what I could do to support myself and have a flexible schedule with my daughter. The probing continued day after day, week after week, month after month. Searching, searching . . . for a sign, an idea, an epiphany, that could lead me in the right direction. For nearly a year and a half, those walks offered hope and respite from the depression that continued to consume me.

Then, one sunny day, my supplications were answered.

As I walked along in my daily routine, I suddenly heard a loud male voice: "Sell your granola." My body jolted and I stopped in my tracks, trying to understand what had happened. I looked around, but no one was near. Feeling a bit silly, I asked out loud, "What did you say?" The voice repeated, calmly but firmly: "Sell your granola." Whose voice was in my head? My inner psyche? My subconscious? Why was it male, and not female? Was it God or some other divine entity? My mind spinning, I continued my walk.

I had not had a religious upbringing, as my Unitarian parents had decided not to sway their children toward specific spiritual beliefs. Words such as "God" and "spirit" and "divinity" weren't heard much in our household. Most of my friends went to church with their families, but that custom was not part of my life. My mother had been raised Methodist but leaned toward Buddhism. My Dad is Jewish, but those traditions didn't enter my spiritual landscape either. Despite my background, I believe, without a doubt, that divine forces are alive and well in our world.

As intriguing to me that such a clear voice could enter my head, was the intrigue at the *content* of the message. As days turned into weeks, I became obsessed with the idea that perhaps I *should* try to sell my granola. My initial reaction of "What kind of cockamamie idea is *that*?" soon morphed into a consideration of possibilities. I did know how to bake granola. I'd been making the cereal since middle school, using a recipe my mom had gotten from a neighbor. It was a wholesome, hippie-era holdout from the '60s, and I never strayed from it.

Over the years, my granola had become such a hit with family and friends that it was the most requested gift for birthdays and holidays. Schoolmates regularly came over for a bowl. By my senior year, it had replaced the usual fast food as my lunchtime staple. I knew I made great granola, but to turn its creation into a business had never occurred to me. Nor had it ever been suggested to me—until that voice showed up.

I had no business background. My degrees were a bachelor's in history and a master's in Spanish—neither of which had introduced me to business classes. My career had consisted of writing and teaching Spanish. Though my work at the chamber exposed me to business ideas, networking opportunities, and classes, it was difficult to picture myself as a businesswoman, much less an entrepreneur.

Although the voice I heard that day was unmistakable, I resisted the idea. I thought it risky to put the wellbeing of myself and my daughter on the line. Natalie was just four, and there had already been significant changes in her life. But as much as I tried to put it out of my head, the idea of starting a granola company became a dragon that would not be tamed. I spent countless nights tossing and turning, wondering if I could pull it off and where I would start. During those sleepless nights, I reminded myself that I had been baking granola since I was fourteen. How hard could it be to bake enough to sell to others?

Two forces worked their spell on my psyche. One, insomnia. It didn't take too many nights to realize why sleep deprivation is used as a torture technique. My daily routine felt heavy, with the lack of sleep adding to my mental melee. I passed many hours in a zombie state, thoughts passing my mind like flour through a sieve. But despite the brain fog, the idea of starting a business persisted.

The second force working on me was another voice in my head; it was my own saying, "I don't want to be on my death bed wondering, *What if?* What if I had started a granola company? Would it have succeeded? Would I have had employees, my own kitchen? Would it have been local, or something larger? Would I have created other products?" These questions, and others like them, pounded at me and played their part in keeping me awake.

The despair I felt during Natalie's absences gave me the strength to think seriously about making such a change. I knew that if I worked for myself, I could schedule my hours around her activities, instead of the other way around. My stable job and stable income, while attractive for many reasons, couldn't offer the flexibility I needed. Giving up vacation days to go on class field trips or to stay home if she was sick, was taking its toll. So was not having the luxury to spend time with her at school, which was encouraged and which she loved.

Between my work schedule, her school schedule, my parenting schedule, and her sleeping schedule, we didn't have a lot of time together. Not only was I missing out on much of her life, but a good part of my life was dictated by someone else. The nights and weekends without her were brutal.

I'd cry myself to sleep wondering what she'd worn to school, which art projects she'd chosen, what she'd eaten and what stories had been read. I became obsessed with details such as which games she'd played, which songs had been sung, and how she'd spent her quiet time. On the days I didn't see her, I felt cut off.

My most prized possession was accessible only half the time, which caused my pendulum to swing out of balance. If I made my own schedule, at least I could visit her at school, even if it wasn't one of "my" days.

Then, one October night, my decision became clear: If I ever wanted to enjoy sound asleep again, and have flexible hours with my daughter, I had better start a granola company. The following day, I stepped into my boss's office. "I came to tell you I'm quitting," I told her as I sat down. Her eyes doubled in size. "Is something wrong? Have you found other work?"

"No," I replied, "I'm starting a granola company."

After a moment of disbelief, she took a deep breath and asked, "A granola company? Do you have any experience running a business?"

"No."

"Have you found a bakery?"

"No."

"Do you have a business plan?"

"No."

"A marketing plan?"

"No."

"Well, certainly you've researched what granolas are on the market and what kind of competition they'll be."

"Not yet."

"Have you thought about the packaging?"

"Not really."

"What about pricing?"

"I haven't gotten that far."

"Well, where do you plan to sell your granola?"

When I said I didn't know that either, she gave up. Her point had been made. Although the conversation made me realize how much I didn't know, and hadn't even considered, I had no intention of changing my mind.

My boss convinced me to finish out the year part-time. I'm not sure if this was mainly for the chamber's benefit or if she was thinking about a safety net for me, just in case things didn't work out. I would have three months to test the waters. We left the door open in case I had a change of heart.

For the next three months, I worked at the chamber in the morning, then went home to work on the business. I was starting from Ground Zero, and the learning curve was steep. My "to do" list grew steadily. My priorities: find ingredient suppliers, packaging suppliers, a graphic designer, an accountant, and, most important, a bakery. The hours flew by. Suddenly I found myself working eighty hours a week: twenty for the chamber, and another sixty for myself, doing my best to figure things out. Fortunately, many of those hours consisted of things that could be done after Natalie had gone to bed. On the days I had her, for the most part, I set work aside during her waking hours.

Then there was the small detail of sharing the news with my parents. For the most part, we had a friendly relationship; I didn't know how they would react, but I figured they would support me as best they could, and perhaps even like the idea. They had happily eaten my granola for years, and they knew others enjoyed it as well. Still, I was nervous they might not be too receptive to my plan.

One day, needing a break from work, I decided the time had come to share the news. I called and found them both at home. They each got on the line, and I asked them to sit down—something I'd never done before except when I announced my pregnancy. I had their attention. I took a deep breath and said, "I called to tell you I'm quitting my job to start a granola company."

There was a brief silence, which I interpreted as confusion and possible disbelief. Then my mother said, "You're going to start *what*? A *granola* company? However did you come up with that idea? And how do you plan to make a living at it?" Although my mother had generally been supportive of my off-the-grid ideas, this one did not appeal to her. Her concern was clear, and she didn't hide it. My father, on the other hand, offered only silence. He was probably in shock, perhaps with feelings he couldn't articulate. "I've already given notice at work," I added, "and I don't intend to change my mind." Still no response. "Dad," I asked, "are you going to say something?" Silence. "Your father has left the room," my mother told me. "I better get off the phone and see how he's doing."

My father was never keen to talk about his feelings. He had a taciturn nature when it came to anything personal, and that was accepted in our family. He was funny, likeable, and witty, with a dry but keen sense of humor. But when it came to expressing his feelings, he became aloof and non-communicative. He wanted the best for his family, but he didn't know how to express his affection. He worked hard to provide for us, but in doing so, didn't spend much time getting to know us. Usually at his desk, never far from his numbers, he dedicated his time and energy to science and the stock market, his two great passions. We had dinner as a family, took wonderful summer vacations, and spent most Sunday evenings with my grandparents. They had chosen to live nearby to be close to my father, their only child, and to see their grandchildren grow up.

My father's nature was understandable. He and my grandparents had narrowly escaped the Holocaust, but only after my grandfather had spent time in Buchenwald. He had been released, and the family's escape out of Germany was equally extraordinary. For my father, processing his past meant reliving that pain; instead, he buried those memories. He was only four when they escaped from Germany and got to England. It took another year to cross over to the United States—thanks to cousins on my grandmother's side who could pay for the voyage and place them in a Quaker community in Vermont, which offered peaceful refuge and a new start.

My father was clearly devoted to his family and our well-being. Still, it was easy to interpret his reticent nature as indifference. I felt detached from him, and the distance felt real. I didn't know how to forge a close bond, so I welcomed the time he did offer and knew that might be as good as it got.

When the granola bomb fell, it didn't fall lightly. My father was not pleased, and through his silence, he let me know it. Although I had never questioned my father's love for me, that silence was as hard as any rejection could have been. Our brief conversations in the weeks that followed were stilted and uncomfortable. He made clear in no uncertain terms that I was being irresponsible, impulsive, unreasonable, and hasty with my decision. He made a valid point that my current job supported my life as a single mom: set hours, a short commute, enjoyable work, and a built-in social life through the many chamber functions I attended. He couldn't understand why I would give all that up to take a huge risk starting a company, especially with no business background. I'm sure he also worried about Natalie. What would become of his beloved granddaughter if I wasn't successful? Would I risk losing my share of her custody if I had no income to support myself? Would I come to him asking for money? Would I lose my townhouse if I couldn't make the mortgage payments? I'm sure these thoughts and more ran through his head, but what he mostly expressed was silence.

Although my father was hesitant to believe I could make a living from my endeavor, he said that if I were going to go through with it, I needed to figure out my numbers. Not just costs, but what I would need to charge to make a profit. Realizing my mind was made up, he offered to help.

I sent him wholesale prices for ingredients and packaging, and my estimates for labor and kitchen rental. I hadn't yet calculated costs for liability insurance, manufacturing fees, wholesale and retail licenses, graphic design, delivery charges, and other expenses. We began with nuts-and-bolts operating costs, bare bones and on a shoestring budget. About a week later, he emailed me his conclusions. With a bit of trepidation, and a skipped heartbeat, I read them.

The report was very business-like, summarizing the results of his calculations. He began with the pro, which consisted of three sentences: "The product is outstanding. Most people who have tasted Fiona's All-Natural Granola say it is the best they have ever eaten. Based on this nearly unanimous, very positive, feedback, one is encouraged to proceed with a plan to produce and market this product." The cons made up the rest of the report, consisting of four full pages of analysis. Primarily, the cons spelled out what he considered to be prohibitively high costs for labor, packaging, fixed expenses, and marketing fees. Other cons were production capacity limitations, regulatory concerns, and high wholesale and retail prices, both for bulk and packaged granola.

My father's conclusions, which consisted of six sections, began: "This project appears to be unviable. The product, while of very high quality, seems too expensive, and probably can neither be produced nor sold in sufficient quantities to generate an adequate income for the proprietor. The cost estimates used in this analysis may well be too low, but even with these numbers, success is extremely doubtful."

His report ended: "This analysis concludes that this project should be terminated as expeditiously as possible, without incurring further expenses. While this recommendation will be disappointing to the proprietor, if followed it will prevent further and larger financial losses and disappointments later. This recommendation is also disappointing to this analyst, who had hoped to be able to predict a positive outcome for this project. Unfortunately, the numbers seem to preclude such a result."

My father's analysis was intended to be unbiased and objective. However, I didn't see it that way. Although he had done his best with my numbers, his conclusions were unacceptable. I took his report personally and felt hurt. It was clear he did not support my endeavor, and thus did not support me in my efforts. I knew him well enough to understand it would be hard to win him over.

Not only was I angry but I was also offended. I took his findings as a personal affront to my abilities. I interpreted his report as a lack of belief in both my competence and my potential. After much fuming, more silence, and a widening gap between us, I decided there was only one course of action: Prove him wrong. I passionately believed in my mission, had heard positive feedback from others, and was feeling happier than I had in a long time. My hours without Natalie were consumed as I researched each aspect of the business. Happily, my granola world engulfed me and kept my spirits afloat. Contacts I'd made via the chamber served me well. Although I didn't know any food entrepreneurs, I did know accountants, commercial real estate agents, corporate lawyers, graphic designers, and marketing professionals—all of whom I would use at one point or another.

I was soon communicating solely with my mother. She had raised her children full-time, and had some idea of how emotionally painful my days without Natalie were. This helped her be sympathetic to my cause—understanding, as a stay-at-home mom, the importance of that close contact.

Not seeing Natalie first thing in morning left me feeling vacant all day. When she wasn't with me, my mind constructed all the facets of her routine that I had come to love: picking out her clothes, helping with breakfast, and choosing her next book and art project. At night, I imagined our bedtime routine: putting on her jammies, brushing her teeth, and chatting about our plans for the next day. I imagined myself by her bed, reading stories and tucking her in with a big kiss and hug. The days without her, I blew kisses and exclaimed, "Good Morning!" and "Good Night!"

Relaying these emotions to my father, a man who equated his love for his family with his ability to provide for them, seemed insurmountable. In his mind, I was acting defiant, immature, and stubborn. I wouldn't listen to reason, nor take his advice. Thus, the standoff began.

My mother was caught in the middle. Like my father, she also doubted I could earn a living by making granola. However, other than her initial reaction to my idea, she refrained from sharing more opinions. Up to that point, no one in our family had questioned my father's skill with numbers. He had earned a Ph.D. in physics from Cal Tech; to question his calculations was unthinkable. And far be it for me, the youngest, to be the first. Yet that is exactly what I did. His unequivocal recommendation that I abandon my idea immediately, before even giving the idea a trial run, only made me more determined to succeed. I set out to prove him—and his numbers—wrong.

~2~
OLD RECIPE, NEW BEGINNINGS

"We become what we give ourselves the power to be."
—Anonymous
(Quote on boxes of Almond Cranberry Granola)

To balance my father's opposition, I received positive feedback and good wishes from people in Boulder. One day, a co-worker at the chamber sent an email: "Fiona, what a wonderful reason to be leaving a job—I wish you the best on your new company and look forward to the yummy samples! It takes a lot of courage and investment in yourself to start your own business, and it's nice to know someone willing to do it. I'm sure you'll be successful!" Another colleague said, "If anyone can do it, *you* can, Fiona." Someone else said, "Fiona, you are so well connected, there's no way you *couldn't* be successful." That kind of encouragement helped me to feel brave about my decision.

One evening, while I was home working on the business, my friend Patricia called. She and I had met at our babysitting co-op, where friendships soon blossomed, both between the two of us and between her son, Gibran, and my daughter, Natalie. The call was to invite me to an event at Planet Bluegrass, a venue in the gorgeous canyon near Boulder where our kids attended preschool.

"Oh Patricia," I told her, "I'm sure it will be a great concert, and I'd love to go! It's just that I've started a granola company, and I have a lot to do."

"A granola company!" she exclaimed. "Wow, what a cool idea. When did you decide to do that?" We talked a bit more, and she convinced me to go to the concert.

Afterward, people gathered to enjoy cocktails and conversation. Some learned that I had started a granola company, and a few replied:

"Whoa!" What a great idea! Boulder should be home to a granola company."

The consensus was that I would meet with great success, and they all said they'd be first in line to buy my granola. One woman asked, "Are you working on your website?"

"My website?" I thought. "Uh, no, not yet," I replied.

"A friend of mine is breaking into the website business, and he might be willing to build your site as a template, since he needs to figure out what it entails." That sounded like a fair trade to me.

When we met for lunch the following week, I immediately felt comfortable with Dylan, the graphic designer. I learned that he was a musician, chef, and visual artist who wanted to expand his artistic skills and enterprises.

"When you give me your logo," he said, "I'll create a theme and design for your website."

That would be challenging, as I didn't have a logo yet. To my delight, I learned that logo creation was one of his specialties.

I had decided to name my company Golden Lotus Granola. I've always baked my granola until golden brown, and I loved the symbolism between the flower and my own life. Every morning, the lotus emerges from dark, muddy waters, and it returns there each night. Each new day, it opens clean, refreshed, and unblemished. Although my own life had become mucky and tarnished with the pain of divorce and reduced time with Natalie, I was determined to find beauty and a fresh start with it all. The lotus flower, since it opens fresh and vibrant each day, is also associated with rebirth—another parallel, since I was embarking on a new journey and giving birth to a new entity. The lotus flower represents detachment, since its roots dangle in the water. I also felt detached from earlier roots.

The lotus flower is associated with spiritual awakening and purity. The divine presence I recognized as I started my company held power for me, and my intentions with starting my company were pure: a flexible lifestyle in which I could make my own schedule as a single mom.

I showed Dylan images of a lotus motif I had found. The flowers were digitized and not attractive, but I loved the composition. Three flowers were set on a background of two lily pads. One was in its bud phase, with a hint that blossoming had begun. Another had just opened, with a few petals separating from the bud. The other was in full bloom. The composition was symbolic to me, as I viewed my journey with the granola company as a way to fully blossom. I instructed Dylan to make the flowers gold, the background blue, and keep the lily pads.

The next time we met, he brought five logo designs. His creative talents had transformed those digitized flowers into artistic representations. One design jumped at me. The lotus flowers formed the center of an oval, which was enveloped by the words *Fiona's All Natural*, in gold writing. A banner held the word *Granola*. The royal blue background was thinly framed in black. When my finger landed on "the one," he smiled. "That's my favorite, too," he said. "I was hoping you would choose it." Shortly thereafter, he incorporated my first tagline: "Organic Goodness in Every Bite!"

In doing my research, I had discovered a Lotus Foods in the United States, and a Golden Lotus rice company in Japan. Registering the name Golden Lotus Granola could be risky. I decided to find a different name and asked just about everyone I spoke with, "What do you think I should name my company?" I described the logo design and explained that I wanted the name to fit with it. In almost every instance, the reply was: "You should name it after yourself!" Or, "Why don't you call it 'Fiona's Granola'? That has such a nice ring to it." Naming the company after myself felt odd. But until I found another name, I couldn't move forward with tasks such as creating business cards and passing out samples.

One morning, I was at my desk at the chamber writing a newsletter when the president strolled by. "So," he asked, "have you chosen a name for your company yet?"

"Nope," I replied sullenly. "Still haven't figured it out."

"Well, it's obvious to me," he answered.

"Oh!" I immediately perked up. "What's that?"

"Fiona's Granola, of course. Not only does it have a nice ring to it, but it tells the world Fiona is a real person who's willing to put her name on her product. That alone says a lot." I told him I'd never thought of it that way.

"Well, look at other food companies that do that. You've got Newman's Own, started by Paul Newman. You've got Annie's pastas, Uncle Eddie's vegan cookies, and Ben and Jerry's ice cream. These people are proud of their products and proud to put their names on what they offer. Fiona is an unusual name and one that isn't heard very often. Plus, 'Fiona's Granola' is very catchy. Think about it."

I decided to go for it. The clock was ticking, and I needed to keep up. My job at the chamber—and my steady paycheck—would soon be over. Turning my granola into a source of revenue would be a necessity. The next day, I registered the name of my company: "Fiona's Natural Foods, doing business as Fiona's Granola."

I was living in Longmont, twelve miles north of Boulder. It was a friendly community, and the commute to work was easy. Life wasn't as diverse or exciting as I imagined Boulder to be, but there were advantages. Housing was more affordable, and business rentals too. Searching for production space, I found a small cafe, the Spelt Berry Bakery, on Main Street on the edge of downtown.

As soon as I met the owner, Elsie, I knew we would get along. Elsie is Puerto Rican. We spoke Spanish together and bonded instantly. Her husband, Ralph, ran the business with her. We arranged for me to use the kitchen at the back of the cafe at night after it had closed. It was small, with an oven only slightly larger than the one I had at home, and little counter space. But there was storage for a few hundred pounds of ingredients, utensils, and bins of finished product. And, unlike the kitchen at home where I produced my granola samples, hers was approved by the Boulder County Health Department.

Not feeling the need to sign a rental agreement, we agreed orally on a monthly fee, and I moved production to her cafe.

Elsie and I enjoyed sharing her space. She had two daughters close to Natalie's age, so sometimes we'd both bring our girls to the bakery. They played while we worked. I loved the opportunity to practice my Spanish, swap granola for her baked goods, and network. We shared distributor information, business ideas, and product ideas. Our relationship was harmonious, splitting the space, utilities, and other expenses. Because of the limited counter space, my packaging had to be done at home. After the granola was baked and cooled, I poured it into large plastic bins and schlepped it to my little townhouse. My personal kitchen there became packaging central, filled with the aroma of freshly baked granola.

I left various samples—Nutty Raisin, Almond Cranberry, Ginger Walnut, Tropical Almond, and others—at groceries, coffee shops, fitness clubs, cafes, and B&Bs. Each Ziploc baggie was labeled with my logo and phone number. By the time orders came in, I hoped, I would have packaging and a timeline to offer. I attended networking functions and other events, and solicited feedback as I passed out the samples.

When I wasn't working at the chamber, I designed labels, sourced supplies, learned about UPC barcodes, and decided on retail packaging, sizes, and pricing. I also educated myself about health claims such as "High in . . ." and "Rich in . . ." to understand what could be stated legally on the packaging.

Top priority was to adjust my tried-and-true recipe and create unique varieties. Going into business, I realized I had to radically transform the recipe from my childhood. Originally, it called for wheat. Although the gluten-free craze hadn't taken hold yet, wheat was a common allergen. My recipe called for dried milk. Dairy allergies were common, and the vegan population in Boulder was on the rise; marketing a product that contained dairy was not a smart business decision. Soy would have to go too, partly because soy crops were often genetically modified, and partly because soy allergies were on the rise. Replacing those protein sources would be a challenge. Adding to my ingredient adventures, the pecans I had always used turned out to be one of the most expensive nuts on the market.

Lastly, I would need to find a substitute for honey. True vegans consider honey an animal product and will not eat it. Pure honey has a high-glycemic index that can cause blood sugar to soar. Finally, because of its thickness and viscosity, it must be heated to integrate easily with the other ingredients. For home baking, that wasn't a big deal, but for a commercial enterprise, it would be a time-consuming extra step.

Reformulating the granola into something I had never baked, yet would be just as healthy and tasty, was a good challenge. Some of the ingredients I kept, such as oats, sesame seeds, and coconut. I developed my base recipe quickly. I was having so much fun with the product development that I soon had more flavors_than any store would be willing to carry. Looking back, some of the varieties were pretty silly: Mixed Nut—that sounds like a good pairing for beer; Mixed Nut 'N Fruit—okay, but what kind of nuts and what kind of fruit? Walnut Papaya—tasty, but natural papaya only came in spears, which needed to be chopped; Walnut Raisin—this because walnuts were my least expensive nut, and raisins my least expensive fruit.

I considered apricots. Those must be chopped, and anyone who's done that knows what a sticky mess it is. Without sulfites—a preservative—dried apricots become brown and shriveled. Not knowing if brown apricots would appeal to the masses, I opted out. As for other ideas, such as cherries and chia seeds, they were cost prohibitive. I soon discovered that my creative side almost always had to take a back seat to the practical side of product development. Although I felt constrained by which ingredients could work price-wise, it was a fun challenge to take the ingredients that were affordable and turn them into something wonderful and memorable.

Because of nut allergies, I decided to offer a nut-free variety. The best description I could come up with was No Nut, which led to the question I heard most often: "So what *does* it contain?" I made that variety coconut-free also, since many people were concerned about coconut's saturated fats. Coconut's health properties are numerous, and its medium-chain fatty acids are extremely beneficial. But convincing the general public of that would be difficult. That variety did not contain fruit either, which made a descriptive title even more challenging. My *No Nut* variety would be the answer for anyone who wanted a granola without nuts, fruit, or coconut.

It didn't take long, though, to realize the name just had to go. I needed to distinguish it in some way, and make that variety at least a little bit exciting. It wasn't selling well, and I suspected part of the reason was the name. After months of brainstorming and continued product development, I hit upon the magic ingredient: orange oil. Someone along the way had turned me on to it, and I loved it. One day I added it to a batch of No Nut. The result was amazing! The entire bakery smelled like essence of orange, and everyone who tried it gobbled it up.

The name for the new variety popped into my head on a bike ride: "Orange Crunch." "*Orange Crunch?*" I thought. "Well, it does have a nice ring to it." I was familiar with the carbonated beverage called Orange Crush but wasn't worried about any confusion. Since I don't watch football, I had no idea it was a nickname for the Denver Broncos and would be taken to refer to the team. For years, customers called that variety Orange Crush. Some people—mostly men—bought it simply because they were Broncos fans and liked the name: "Oh, Orange Crush granola! I'm a Broncos fan. I'll buy some of that."

Years later, the UPC shelf tags used for ordering still read "No Nut," since that was how I'd first gotten the variety into stores. Leaving that unchanged, despite the different name on the packaging, meant I didn't have to face the approval process again for what would have been deemed a new cereal. No harm done, and sales skyrocketed once the granola went from No Nut to Orange Crunch. What's in a name? Sometimes, everything.

* * *

Dylan had created a wonderful logo, but his learning curve with the website was high, and the task was taking longer than we had planned. One night, I went to a party hosted by someone in natural products. I met Brad, a graphic designer specializing in websites. His focus was the natural products industry, including food. Calm and competent, his easygoing nature put me at ease. We met at his office the following week and discussed concepts and the general look and feel I had envisioned, as well as content and color scheme. By the time I left, I knew my website was in good hands.

Brad and I spent a lot of time together those next couple of months, creating the pages and tweaking the design and layout. I had decided to make the website educational and fun and enlisted my mother to help. I attended to the nutritional aspects while she focused on colorful facts. My favorite was the origin of the term "Open Sesame!" In the children's tale "Ali Baba and the Forty Thieves," Ali Baba discovers he can enter a thieves' treasure den with the words "Open sesame!" The phrase came about because of the way the pods burst open with a pop, much like the sudden pop of a lock. It was just the kind of unusual information I enjoyed adding to my site.

For the photos, I hired a photographer I knew from the chamber. He came to our townhouse, where I had arranged bowls of ingredients, granola, fruit, and place settings. He photographed the ingredients, and Natalie and me eating granola. We enjoyed the photo shoot.

Diligence and long days paid off. Soon my site was up, and I loved it. Brad had done a fantastic job with the design, and I was happy with the copy. The website began: "At Fiona's All-Natural Granola, we believe good nutrition is the cornerstone for a healthy body, mind, and spirit." The homepage included a personal welcome statement and described how the granola was lovingly baked to crispy, golden perfection in small batches using organic ingredients. An adorable picture of Natalie was near the center, smiling and eating a bowl of granola in her favorite dress, with the words: "I love my mommy's granola!" She was four, with long, blonde, curly hair and sharp blue eyes. Although she didn't understand what a website was, she was pleased to see her smiling face whenever I opened it. The home page included the logo, a photo of three sizes of bags, and my first testimonial: "Eating Fiona's Granola is a life-altering experience!"

On other pages, readers learned the history and inspiration behind the company and what distinguished my granola from other brands. We included nutritional information and a recipe for granola/fresh fruit/yogurt parfaits, photographed in crystal champagne glasses inherited from my great aunt. The agave was featured in a clear glass bowl my grandmother had brought from Europe. We suggested different ways to enjoy the granola, solicited feedback, and included a photo of Natalie and me at the breakfast table. We listed the retail locations: granola was available in six local towns at coffee shops, cafes, restaurants, and a frozen yogurt shop. The last page offered a Chinese proverb: "Words are mere bubbles, but deeds are drops of gold." Adding personal touches to the website was important to me, as was involving Natalie, since she was the reason I had started the company.

My business was expanding quickly, as was Elsie's. After just a few months, it was time to find a bakery with a bigger production area and more storage space. Since most of my accounts were in were in Boulder, as was Natalie's preschool, it made sense to find bakery space there.

A month into my search, I found a large, two-story warehouse in Boulder that was home to a catering company. The proprietor, who baked bread and cooked for his events, rented space to a flax cracker company run by a few happy hippies, a dumpling company owned by three Taiwanese sisters, and a burrito company. There was one additional space available, upstairs. I could bake and package downstairs, at night, but the storage would be upstairs. Not ideal, but it seemed better than my current situation. I agreed to his terms, gave notice to Elsie, and moved operations two weeks later.

With nonstop food preparation, humidity and savory aromas filled the building. The upstairs was always warm. My safflower oil, which I'd switched to when sunflower oil became unavailable, often turned rancid; many unused jugs ended up in the trash.

Another problem was the narrow, steep, and slippery staircase leading to my space. Our boxes and bags of ingredients were heavy, as were the filled bins of granola. I slipped many times hauling product up and down. Because of the warmth, sometimes the cooled granola became heated, which caused it to become soft and moist; we had to retoast it to make it crispy and dry again. Precise timing was key: I packaged as soon as possible after the granola had cooled, before it might get warm and soft again, then immediately hauled it out, either to accounts or to my townhouse in Longmont, where it would stay cool and dry and crispy. So much for my idea to quit hauling granola between Longmont and Boulder.

Next issue: my baker. Until I moved operations to Boulder, I had done the baking and packaging myself. With the business expanding, I couldn't do production along with everything else required to manage and grow my company.

Carlos made burritos during the day but was available at night. He insisted the two shifts wouldn't be too much. The burrito company owner said Carlos was his best employee, and I liked the fact that I could speak Spanish with him. He gave me a nine-digit number that looked like a social security number and said he was legal. Other companies had used his number without problem. I took my chances.

Carlos was a good worker, when he wanted to be. Some days he was punctual, respectful, and baked granola the way I had trained him. Other days, he didn't show up for his shift. Sometimes, he'd burn the granola until it was almost black. I'd climb those slippery steps, open the bins, and discover charred granola. "Aaargh! Carlos!" I'd cry out, not caring who heard. "You burned the granola again!" Occasionally I'd hear snickers. I'd storm downstairs to let him have it, in English. I usually spoke Spanish with Carlos, but cursing was not my forte. I had translated all the recipes for him, so he understood the baking technique and temperatures just fine.

Carlos always had an excuse: The oven wasn't holding the right temperature, the buzzer was broken, he was tired, his car had broken down, there was an emergency in his family, or he forgot he was supposed to come in. Sometimes he claimed the granola wasn't burnt and that I was being too particular. If it wasn't overly brown, I took it to the women's shelter. Otherwise, into the trash it went. My accounts occasionally had to wait an extra day for their deliveries, and we'd have to double production on the following shift to make up for lost granola.

As if my production woes weren't problematic enough, Carlos made passes at me. He flirted, asked me out, and got too close for my comfort zone. My rote response was, "Carlos, I'm your boss. Quit flirting with me, and quit asking me out. And start baking better granola!" Carlos didn't last long—his antics and erratic baking were not worth the stress. When our paths crossed in the bakery, we were cordial, and he held no grudge. I used Craigslist to find his two replacements, both as a safety net in case one didn't work out and to cover absences.

The burrito company was owned by a couple who no longer lived together, but they co-owned the business. Len ran their production operations, and Jill managed the deliveries. They sold and distributed their burritos statewide. In addition to the burritos, Jill delivered products for other companies. Since my business was expanding, I hired her to deliver for me. She covered all my Colorado sales except Boulder, Longmont, and three neighboring towns, where I managed the deliveries.

After I replaced Carlos and hired Jill, operations ran more smoothly, but other problems continued. I worried employees would slip on those stairs and sue me, or present a liability claim. The heat upstairs continued to be an issue. After throwing away yet one more jug of safflower oil, I switched oils. After considering olive, soybean, vegetable, hemp, grapeseed, and coconut oils, I switched to canola. New to the market, it was shelf stable, inexpensive, had a neutral flavor, and withstood high baking temperatures. At least for the time being, my oil problems were solved.

I had decided on pricing with my father's help, based on the spreadsheets he created. Although still concerned about my decision to start the company, he was aware of the growing popularity and increased sales. His spreadsheets incorporated production, ingredient, packaging, and overhead costs. Although Fiona's was more expensive than other granolas, it was the only one made locally. My line was organic and the flavors unique, and the packaging stood out. The golden chunks of granola, visible through the bag and set off by the lotus flower motif, made an attractive display.

Initially, I listed quantities in terms of cups and ounces. Since we put either one, five, or seven cups of granola in a bag, listing the quantity by cups seemed perfectly logical to me. The gram requirement was one I found out about in February 2002, when I landed my first grocery account. Lorraine, a business astrologer I'd met at a chamber event, knew the grocery buyer at the local Vitamin Cottage and told me I should bring her a bag of granola. "Seriously, Fiona, this is the best granola I have ever eaten. Puja will love it, and you'll land your first grocery account. Trust me."

I did trust her. We had agreed to barter granola for astrology readings. I'd always been interested in astrology but had never pursued it. I was curious to see my natal chart and gain a sense of what might lie ahead for the business. For our first session, I went to her house with five "five-cup" bags of granola we'd agreed on for an astrology reading. I had already given her my date and place of birth, so she had my chart prepared.

We sat down, and she looked at me intently. "So, Fiona," she began. "I want you to look at these stones and sand on the table and imagine them as boulders in a flowing river. The boulders represent the obstacles you'll face as you proceed with your company. As you can see, there are quite a few. But as you can also see, the river wends its way around and over these boulders. I'll be honest and not sugarcoat anything. You'll face many obstacles. But with perseverance, you'll overcome them and meet with great success. The journey will not be an easy one, and it will test every ounce of your patience and purpose." She paused, and I took a deep breath. "Now, let's begin with the first obstacle. The first boulder I see is your father. Your relationship with him has been tested over the years. Tell me about that."

"My *father*?" I asked. "You can see *him* in my chart?"

"Of course I can," she replied. "Your relationship with him hasn't been easy, has it? I see a lot of stress surrounding money and your father. That needs to be worked out. But I see great success with your business, great success. But you've got to deal with these issues."

I told her he had always provided for us but had not been available emotionally. When I'd expressed interest in fields such as marine biology and anthropology, he'd said he didn't feel they were suitable careers for a woman who would want to raise a family, since I might be out at sea or in the field for extended lengths of time. My father encouraged higher education for his son and daughters alike. He never suggested we apply for loans or work during college. He generously dished out funds to pay for each of our undergraduate degrees, letting us focus on our studies and not worry about paying back student loans. My two siblings chose New Mexico State University, which offered fields they wanted, let them stay near friends in the area, and come home to Alamogordo to do laundry and eat a homemade meal.

But I couldn't decide. I felt ready to explore a different part of the country. I had already spent a year doing social service work in Europe, partly to satisfy my never-ending wanderlust and partly because I hoped it would help me decide on a field of study. When I returned—bilingual, well-traveled, and twenty-five pounds heavier—I still had no clue what to do with my life.

The next year, I lived at home and attended the local branch of NMSU. My father urged me to pursue a liberal arts education. "It will prepare you for anything," he said. "You'll be introduced to different subjects and ideas, and something will call out to you." He pushed his alma mater, Grinnell College in Iowa. "It's small, friendly, and one of the best colleges in the country. I'm sure my degrees from Grinnell are what got me into Cal Tech. Think about it."

I thought about it. "*Iowa? Really?* How can I be apart from my beloved mountains? How can I trade them for corn fields?" In addition to the lack of hiking opportunities, I worried that Iowa might be politically conservative. Moreover, the thought of long, cold winters and heavy humidity didn't appeal to me. I just couldn't picture myself living in Iowa.

A couple months after our conversation, my father was invited to give a speech at Grinnell. He was one of the college's most noted alumni, partly because he had been accepted into NASA's astronaut program as a payload specialist, which brought a bit of fame with it, and partly because he was a keen supporter of the school.

"Why don't you come with me?" he suggested. "You can stay in a dorm and get a feel for what student life would be like."

Though I'd written off the idea of living in Iowa, I hadn't told him just yet. I hesitated. "Dad, I really don't think I'm interested in Grinnell. I'm sure it's a fine school, but I'm not thrilled with the idea. I'd miss the mountains too much, and I don't think I'd tolerate the wet winters too well. I hope you're not offended."

He told me I wasn't thinking about the most important aspects of an education. "You'll be inside studying most of the time anyway," he replied. "And there are so many extracurricular activities, you probably won't feel the need to leave campus very often. I think you should reconsider."

With a bit of reluctance, I agreed to visit Grinnell with my dad, partly to appease him and partly to decide soon or face another year at the local NMSU. Long story short, I felt comfortable immediately. Surrounded by a hilly, fertile landscape, the campus is attractive and filled with friendly students and faculty; I had pleasant encounters with both. I found the student body to be liberal, diverse, international, and imaginative.

At one point, my dad introduced me to John Pfitsch, the athletic director, still at Grinnell some thirty years after my dad attended. As a school statistician, my father had traveled with the football and basketball teams under the tutelage of Coach Pfitsch, and they had formed a lasting friendship.

"You'll love it here at Grinnell," John said. "Not only will you be a double chip, but you'll find the students to be quite gregarious." I had no idea what a double chip was, nor what "gregarious" meant.

"Uh, yeah," I replied. "Sounds good!"

I learned that a "double chip" was a student with a parent who'd graduated from Grinnell. The term gregarious—I looked that one up. And John was right. The students were gregarious. I completed my college years at Grinnell, changing majors three times before settling on history, the only area in which I had enough credits to graduate in four years. Although I didn't pursue a career in history, I enjoyed my years at Grinnell. And I had to hand it to my dad: The degree did open doors for me. I also made lasting friendships and received a top-notch education along the way.

Although my father knew I'd gotten a good education, he was still opposed to the idea that I continue my granola business. That first session, I told Lorraine his prognosis for the company. "He already tried to talk me out of doing this," I told her. "It's much more of an uphill battle without his confidence than I ever thought it would be."

"Well," she replied, "have no worries. You'll be wildly successful, and eventually you'll win him over." I told her that despite his disapproval of the idea, he was dedicating quite a bit of time to help me with the numbers. "I do believe he wants me to succeed. He just can't imagine that people will pay what I'll have to charge for this granola." She reminded me that in Boulder, people are happy to pay top dollar for healthy, organic products. "Take what he can offer, and you'll have to figure out the rest without him," she advised.

Before I left that afternoon, she gave me a hug. She'd already called Puja. "She can't wait to try the granola. Get some over to her as soon as you can."

That was easy for her to say. She had no idea how unprepared I was. I hadn't finished pricing the five-cup bags or obtained the UPC codes. I was still printing labels on my ink jet and hadn't upscaled the recipes for larger runs. Our production capacity was limited, which added to my hesitation to enter a regional grocery chain.

Earlier that fall, I had obtained nutrition labels from the food analysis lab at the University of Northern Colorado. Software for nutritional analyses did exist, but it was expensive. I had no plans to develop more products, so it seemed logical not to invest in software I would use only once.

The lab required five pounds of product. I had the option to ship the granola or personally deliver it. Always curious, I asked if I could witness the process. "It's not that interesting," the lab technician answered, "but you're welcome to check it out." When I told my boss I needed to take a day off to have the granola analyzed, she smiled and said, "Well, I hope the winds aren't blowing too hard." I laughed and agreed. Her comment referred to the cattle industry in northern Colorado. When the winds are strong, the smell of manure is intense.

I got lucky the day I went up; the winds were down. First, the technician ground the granola. Then she divided it into equal parts—the instruments tested carbohydrates, calories, fat, protein, sodium, and other components. The machines chugged along and results were fed into a computer.

A week later, the information arrived in the mail. I had always wondered about the nutritional composition of my granola; after twenty-three years of baking, I finally found out.

Since Lorraine had given the granola rave reviews, and promised Puja I would drop off a sample, I called Vitamin Cottage. When she came to the phone, I introduced myself and asked if she'd allow me to bring in a bag. "Of course!" she replied. "Lorraine can't say enough wonderful things about your granola. I can't wait to try it." We set up a meeting for the next day.

When Puja laid her eyes on the granola, she broke into a smile. "Lorraine was right!" she exclaimed. "This granola looks delicious, the packaging is attractive, and I just love this logo."

Then she inspected the bag. "Sooo," she asked, "what's the weight in grams?" I stared at her, dumbfounded.

"The weight in grams? Is that important?"

"In the grocery world, we don't go by volume. We go by weight. You'll need to state both ounces and grams on your label. And, no cups," she added with a smile.

To weigh the bags, I was using a postage scale inherited from my grandmother, which only displayed ounces. Who cares how many grams are in a bag of granola?" I wondered. But that was the regulation, so off I went to find a digital scale that also displayed grams. I learned there are 454 grams to a pound, and 28.375 grams to an ounce.

The next afternoon, Puja called. "Fiona, this is by far the best granola I have ever eaten. And I'm very particular when it comes to granola. How soon can you get some over here?" Before I could answer, she added, "I'll send it down to corporate with a recommendation that Debbie, our corporate grocery buyer, approve it. She'll be concerned about the price; it'll be the most expensive granola on the shelf. But it's organic and it's local, and if she likes it half as much as I do, I think she'll approve it."

"Honestly, Puja," I had to answer, "I don't think I'm ready for this. I'm sure I could supply a few stores, but I don't even have the barcodes generated yet. How's the granola supposed to scan at the registers?"

"Oh, I didn't realize you don't have barcodes yet. Hmmm." Puja paused, then went on. "Okay, so get those as soon as possible. But I don't want that to hold things up. For now, assuming the granola is approved, we'll put a price sticker on the bags when you come in. Even if Boulder is the only store you get into for now, that's fine. It lets us see how it sells and gives you time to get the codes generated.

"Because of the price and the fact it's a brand-new product with very little sales history, I'm sure Debbie won't automatically place it in all the stores. But once you get approval, you can approach each store individually. Sound good?"

A little overwhelmed, I told her yes, it sounded good. With that, we hung up.

Two weeks later, Puja called: "Great news, Fiona! Debbie has approved your granola. How soon can you get me six units of each variety?" I would have three feet of shelf space, quite generous for a new product that was high end and had little sales history. We had already agreed on pricing: $5 per bag wholesale, with the store charging $7.49 after markup. Steep, but maybe not too steep for a pound and a half of local, organic granola.

Debbie recommended it the grocery buyers as a new item but warned it would be the most expensive they offered; time would tell if customers were willing to pay it.

That was February 2002. I had been working full time for my company since quitting my chamber job at the end of December as planned.

Although I was putting in long days, including weekends, I controlled where, when, and for how long I worked. I was learning to delegate. I no longer baked, and I packaged only occasionally. During the waking hours Natalie shared with me, I worked as little as possible. A few times a week, we stopped by the bakery to check in with employees or pick up product. We enjoyed chatting with the workers from other companies, and Natalie helped herself to baked goods. We did deliveries together, and she got to know employees on a first-name basis; they all enjoyed interacting with her. Whatever the task, we turned it into a fun outing.

Natalie loved socializing. Her adorable manner drew people to her, and she enjoyed their attention. At home, I did my best to keep our together time granola-free. Once she was tucked in, I went back to work. Though I was putting in twice as many hours as at the chamber, my new career didn't feel like work. It was an adventure. Every day was different; every day I met new people and learned something new, and every day, the hours flew by. In a short time, I had gone from continual heartache on the days Natalie wasn't with me to keeping so busy that the next thing I knew, she was back in my arms again. I still yearned for her when she was with her father, but instead of popping the cork on a bottle or taking a draw from my pipe, I was busy with my next project. The day I found out about Vitamin Cottage, Natalie was with me, and I shared the news. "That's great, Mommy!" she exclaimed. "I'll bet lots of people buy your granola." I told her I hoped she was right, and that I was keeping my fingers crossed.

~3~
FARMERS MARKET: A FRESH ADVENTURE

"Becoming intoxicated with a dream gives us the passion to bring it into reality."

—Kazuo Inamori, Japanese businessman

Earlier, when I was at the catering facility, I had gotten into the Boulder County Farmers Market. I was taking chamber workshops and seminars, knowing how much more I needed to learn about marketing, accounting, and the legal aspects of my business. Quite a bit of buzz had been generated about the decision to quit my job and start a granola company. One day, a classmate learned I was starting a granola company. "That's so cool!" she said. "I'm starting a produce delivery service. Maybe we should talk."

Her name was Christine. She had a bubbly personality and a huge smile, and she seemed as enthusiastic about her business as I was about mine. We exchanged cards and met for tea the following week.

"Guess what?" she asked. "I've just been accepted into the Boulder County Farmers Market to sell fruits and vegetables. I'm so excited! You should apply as well!"

"The *what*?" I answered. I had not been exposed to farmers markets, so they were not places I frequented.

"The farmers market!" she repeated. "Don't tell me you've never gone there."

"No, I guess I haven't."

"Well, I think it would be a great venue for your granola. And the market starts two weeks from Saturday, so if you want to get in, you'd better hop on it."

"Two weeks from Saturday?" I thought. That gave me two weeks and

a day to pull everything together. What the heck, I thought. It could
be a fabulous opportunity.

I called the market manager. "Hello, is this Brenden?"

"Yes, who's this?"

"My name is Fiona, and I've just started a granola company. I realize
this is last minute, but I wonder if there's a chance you'd let me participate in the market this year." A brief silence followed.

"A granola company?" he asked. "That sounds pretty cool! We've
never had a granola company at market as far as I know. I like it. This
is Boulder, after all. There should be granola at the farmers market!"

He asked about ingredients, varieties, if I had other products, where
my bakery was, and a few other questions. "Well," he said, "I have to
check with the board. Since you're not a farmer, you won't have priority with any remaining slots. But I think we can make room for you.
Would you be ready to go in two weeks?" I would have to buy a ten-
by-ten-foot tent, banner, tables, and stool, as well as calculate my pricing, get a retail sales tax license, create signage, buy a money belt, and
stock up on quarters, $1 bills, $5 bills, and $10 bills.

My company was rapidly expanding, which meant free time was already at a minimum. The farmers market sounded like a great idea from
a business perspective, but I had Natalie to think about. The market was
8 a.m. to 2 p.m. Saturdays and 10 a.m. to 2 p.m. Wednesdays. It took
twenty minutes to get there from my home and another hour to set up.

Natalie was only four. She was delightfully easygoing and had
adapted well to going back and forth between her two homes. She got
up early Monday through Friday, and spent time at the bakery and in
the stores. She attended gymnastics and dance class, piano lessons,
birthday parties, and an occasional play date. We swam at the rec center
and at our townhouse. Because she had such a busy life, I thought
she might resent having to wake up early on half her Saturdays.

The opportunity was a good one, but I didn't want to take advantage of her relaxed nature and positive attitude. Even though she'd
need to wake up early, I thought she might enjoy the farmers market.
I assumed other vendors had children there, and I thought it would
be an interesting way to spend our Saturdays.

During the seven months of market, from the first Saturday in April through the first Saturday in November, thousands of customers strolled through, including tourists and business owners—many of them in the food industry. Market would offer wonderful exposure for my granola, and it would augment my social life.

The luxury to hang out and socialize was not part of my new routine. I was constantly on the go and came home exhausted every day, just to work more hours until falling into bed. To sit and watch the world go by twice a week, interacting with customers and passersby, appealed to me a great deal. In addition, like-minded people filled the market: local producers, organic farmers, and customers who supported local vendors. Any following I gained would increase the chance of getting my granola into more stores, since those customers would want the granola year-round.

The day after I had spoken to the market manager, he called. "Fiona, I have good news. You're in! That means you have two weeks. Let me know what I can do to help." After asking where I could purchase a tent, I told him there was one other detail. "I'm a single mom with a four-year-old daughter. Half the Saturdays, she'd come along. If that isn't possible, I won't be able to be a vendor." "Of course you can bring your daughter, Fiona!" he replied. "Many of the vendors have children. I think your daughter will really enjoy it." His answer was music to my ears.

The next day, Natalie returned to my house. During dinner, I brought up the topic and described what it would entail. I didn't sugarcoat it, but I offered a positive spin. "I think it will be fun for both of us, honey," I added. She thought about it and replied, "Okay, Mommy! It sounds good to me. Will there be goodies at market?" I had no idea what food offerings we'd find, but I assured her there would be. She probably hoped market would be filled with the kinds of goodies I didn't allow in the house. If she was open to market, I'd be open to treats along the way.

Relieved at Natalie's seal of approval, I got organized. I drove to Denver to visit Captain Canopy, a jolly fellow who in fact resembled a ship captain. Stout and ruddy-faced, he had a lively sense of humor and a quick wit. In two seconds, he sized me up.

"You'll be needing a lightweight tent. I have just the one for you, in white and royal blue." I chose the blue, which was almost the exact color of my logo background. I ordered a banner, obtained my tax forms and retail sales tax license, and bought three card tables. For table cloths, I used three scarves I had bought in Europe when I was eighteen; they were in surprisingly good shape. I was determined not to spend more money than necessary. My chair would be a barstool that was sitting unused in the basement.

That first Saturday, Natalie was with her dad, which helped me to efficiently scope out the scene, unload, park, and set up by opening bell. Sales were swift.

"Oh, a granola company! I've always thought there should be granola at market."

"Oh, is this your company? How exciting to have local granola in Boulder!"

Customers had a lot of questions, and no one balked at the prices. A few recognized me from the chamber or from Natalie's school. My very first customer owned one of the largest natural product companies in Boulder. He knew me from the chamber and was intrigued with the granola. He bought two large bags of the Almond variety.

I'd come the first day with a lot of bags, six varieties in three sizes. To my delight, they almost all sold.

That day, I fell in love with market as the street filled with friendly vendors and smiling customers. How had that slice of Boulder eluded me? It was as Brenden had said, truly a family atmosphere. I had a distinct feeling Natalie would also feel at home there.

The next time, she was with me, I described market. "I think you'll like it, honey. Everyone is so friendly. I even discovered a place called Art Stop, where kids do art projects." Her face lit up. Natalie was already quite the artist and tended to keep paper and drawing utensils close.

The following Saturday, I had the car loaded with her favorite blanket, stuffed animals, art supplies, books, and snacks. I "scooped" her out of bed, as instructed. With her good sense of fashion even at an early age, she had already chosen a cute outfit.

"Is today the day we go to market?" she sleepily asked.

"Yes, it is," I answered.

"Oh, goodie, I'm excited!" she replied. After she brushed her teeth and went to the bathroom, I put her in the car seat where she promptly fell back to sleep. Once at market, I unloaded the car, parked it, and carried her to our booth. She remained sleeping for the first half hour. Then she woke up and looked around. People were already making a fuss over her, saying lucky I was to have such an adorable daughter.

Natalie loved market. Her mornings began by choosing her breakfast—a chocolate croissant, scone, cinnamon roll, or fruit pastry. I occasionally talked her into an egg burrito. Those Saturday morning breakfasts became a real treat. Occasionally on a Friday, she'd say, "Mommy, I've already decided what I'm going to have for breakfast tomorrow!"

She loved interacting with customers and other vendors. Our neighbors had two daughters close to Natalie's age. The girls bonded immediately and played together every chance they had.

Most Saturdays, Natalie did projects at Art Stop, just down the street on the steps of the art museum. After about an hour, she'd walk back to our booth with a volunteer, beaming, proudly displaying her art. "Here you go, Mommy! This is for you! Do you like it?" Each was a treasure: a book, a drawing, a painting, a piece of jewelry, often related to the seasons or holidays. Natalie participated in Art Stop for years and always enjoyed it.

The midweek market was aimed at folks who worked in Boulder but lived out of town. They could pop over for lunch and buy goodies to take home. When the Wednesday hours shifted to 4 to 8 p.m., more families were attracted because parents and children could have a night out. There was live music, a beer tent, and food to enjoy. The time change meant Natalie could join me. I'd set up, drive to her school and rush back; we barely had time to return before market opened.

Natalie often saw classmates who came with their parents. Her friends were impressed that her mom owned a granola company and that Natalie helped at the booth. Sometimes they'd hang out with us, and sometimes Natalie walked around with her friends.

Market customers were admirably honest. Occasionally, I'd have to leave my booth to run to the restroom or food court, or walk Natalie down the street. Occasionally, upon my return, product was missing; however, payment was almost always on the table, placed strategically so I would find it. I sometimes discovered a large bag of granola missing, and $10 underneath my vitamin container. Or Natalie would discover two granola bars missing and $5 underneath the energy bar basket. This happened throughout the years. When we next saw the customers who had taken the product, they asked whether we had found the money. Others took product but paid the next time: "You weren't at your booth and I didn't want to leave money on your table. Hope that's okay!"

One of my favorite aspects of market was bartering. I didn't know that was an option until a vendor came to my booth one day and said, "Hey Fiona, how about some broccoli and carrots in exchange for granola?"

Thus, the bartering began. We ate very well during market months —I brought home every imaginable fruit and vegetable, pastries, cheeses, and wine. We also bartered for soap, lotion, and flowers. I often sent Natalie down the street with different sizes and varieties of granola, and she came back arms loaded with the goods we had decided to barter for that day.

Sometimes she'd say, "Mommy, today would you trade granola for peaches?" Or "I'd love dumplings for lunch, and the sisters said I could have a bowl for one of your small bags of granola."

The Taiwanese sisters and I still shared the same catering facility and spent many a Friday night together preparing for market. "Sure, honey," I replied. "But how about bring them two small bags of granola because that's a fair trade." Or "How about bring me a bowl also, and I'll give you a big bag of granola to give them." Through the years, those dumplings remained Natalie's favorite market food.

I was at market when the testimonials started flooding in:

"Your granola goes through our house like water."

"This is simply delicious! You're gonna do great!"

"Congratulations! You make mornings at our house very happy."

"Don't you dare stop making this granola! I don't know what I'd do."

One man in his seventies stopped often to chat at my booth, but he never bought any granola. One day, I asked why he hadn't tried any samples.

"Oh, I'm an old hippie," he replied. "I ate so much granola in the '60s and '70s just the thought of eating it again turns my stomach. No offense, because it looks great."

I laughed. "Oh, come on! One little bite won't hurt you."

He hesitated as he eyed the samples. "Okaaay," he finally replied. "I'll try some." He took one bite, and his face lit up. "Wow!" he exclaimed. "This stuff really is good. Better than any granola I remember." He bought a bag and promptly became one of my most loyal customers.

Another man, François, paid with $2 bills. I have no idea how one person can eat so much granola, but he bought four large bags of Ginger Walnut every two weeks. He'd come to market early and set aside the bags. He had learned that on many occasions, certain sizes and varieties sold out quickly, so he gathered his bounty early. One day I asked him why he always paid with $2 bills. "That's just my mode of doing business," he replied. He was a bit of an eccentric, and we got along great.

When Natalie was at the booth, he gave her a $2 bill—just because. "Here you go, little lady," he'd say. The first day he did it, Natalie's eyes opened wide, and she looked at me questioningly. I told her it was okay. She smiled and thanked him. François called the $2 bills his calling cards. "Good morning, little lady" he'd say. "You ready for your calling card?" I explained to Natalie what a calling card was. She certainly enjoyed receiving them.

To solicit feedback, I brought a survey to market. Customers happily shared their opinions. Most were not excited about raisins. They were *so last decade*. Many, upon seeing the Cinnamon Raisin label, exclaimed, "Raisins! Do you have any granola *without* raisins?" To which I'd point out the five varieties that did not contain raisins. "Have you ever thought about using goji berries or hemp seeds? Those have amazing health benefits!" Those ingredients were packed with nutrients, but they would add significantly to the price of the granola.

To jot down other ideas and suggestions from customers, I kept a notebook at market. I also recorded the testimonials—those were a shot in the arm that kept me energized, especially when the sleep deprivation set in. On those days, I read the testimonials to remind myself how much my customers loved the granola. The accolades truly kept me going.

One evening, a cafe owner called. "Is this Fiona?"

"Yes, who's this?"

"My name is Harry," he replied. His East Coast accent was so thick I thought he said "Henry." He talked fast and with excitement as he described discovering my granola at the local food co-op that day.

"Now, I have to tell you: I am a granola connoisseur," he went on to say. "I've tried every granola out there. And I'm *very* picky. But this granola—your granola—is by far the best I've ever tried. I bought a bag and gobbled the whole thing up. I couldn't stop eating it!"

Then he mentioned the cafe he owned in upstate New York. "Can you ship this stuff out of state?" he asked. I assured him it wouldn't be a problem.

"Oh man, my customers are gonna love this stuff! When can I place my first order?" We arranged all the details, but before we hung up, he paused and asked, "This might sound a little weird, but do you happen to have any granola on hand right now, at your house? I enjoyed it so much I wanted to buy some more, but the co-op is closed. My flight is early tomorrow morning, but if it's not too much bother, I could come over now and buy from you directly."

I hesitated. I was alone, and he was a perfect stranger. Still, he sounded sincere, and he was so enthusiastic about the granola. "I do have some here," I said. "Okay, I guess I could sell you a couple of bags." He thanked me profusely, got directions to my condo, and showed up an hour later. He seemed honored to meet me, and mentioned again how superb the granola was. For many years, Harry remained a loyal customer, and though he tried different varieties, he always went back to Almond Cranberry.

I shared just about everything that happened in the bakery with Natalie, positive and negative. When I was upset, she took my complaints to heart and did what she could to help. One day, I discovered a note she had written on a piece of scrap paper she found in the bakery. It read:

FIONA! ~~Lissen~~ Lisen
Talk to ~~back~~ bakers
about cleaning the
table when it's dirty!

~~Thn~~ Thank you
Natalie your dader Haaaa

She was in first grade when these missives began. Her little notes made me smile, and I was touched she took my frustrations to heart.

Occasionally, my bakers and packagers did not arrive for their shifts. Less product meant we had to alter our delivery schedule and the amount of granola we could bring to market. I shared this with Natalie. One night, she took it upon herself to write a note:

Dear Bakers, from now on if you need to miss a baking shift, please call other bakers to find a replacement. Marck this change on the calendar. Please do not call ~~my~~ me. Only call me if you can not find a replacement. Allow plenty of time to find a nother baker. The same goes for packaging. Thank you!!! Fiona, and Natalie!

Please sine initials ___AC ___JV ___JS ___AL ___KW

Although my bakers and packagers did not enjoy being reprimanded, they told me they enjoyed Natalie's cute and candid notes.

~4~
HAVING FUN WITH TAGLINES

"Forsake inhibitions, and pursue thy dreams."
—Anonymous

I had given my granola the tagline, "Organic Goodness in Every Bite!" But I decided that creating a second slogan would help even more. Not many granolas were truly artisan: organic, hand-crafted, baked in small batches, minimally processed, slowly roasted and not dehydrated, only lightly sweetened using agave instead of refined, high-glycemic sweeteners, and without artificial flavorings or fillers. It was important to convey these differences.

Unexpectedly, help in doing this came one Friday night from my Spanish group, which I'd been attending twice a month since Natalie was six months old. We were a tight-knit group of twenty-five to thirty aficionados of the Spanish language, loyal to our mission of maintaining friendship, community, and fluency.

That night, I'd brought a few dozen Ziploc baggies of granola. I stood on a chair and announced that I had started a granola company. I asked each person to take a baggie or two home, eat it with and without milk or yogurt, and report back to me at our next gathering. They readily agreed.

Later that evening, two members, Jim and José, came up to me and said, "Fiona, we think your idea is fantastic! Maybe we could help you with your business or marketing plan. It would be fun to get involved with a food company this early on. Do you want to meet for drinks some night?" Jim was an engineer, while José was an accountant with a business background. They were bright, enthusiastic, and sincere. "Okay!" I replied.

When we met the following week, I explained my idea for another tagline. The glasses of wine loosened our minds and helped the creativity flow. By the end of the evening, we had it: "I'm perfectly baked!"—with "perfectly" in italic.

My hope was that people who saw it would wonder, "How exactly *is* it perfectly baked?" or "What does she mean by 'perfectly baked'?" and would look at the back label to find out.

Soon I'd created T-shirts. The front displayed the company logo and read: "I'm not just half baked . . ." On the back were the words, "I'm perfectly baked!" with "perfectly" written in squiggles to stand out.

Of course, being "baked" had other connotations, especially in Boulder. Although retail marijuana was not yet legal in Colorado, the town held true to its reputation as a liberal, pot-smoking community, home to many hippies. For marketing and to build good relations, I offered the shirts to employees of the stores that sold Fiona's Granola. They were a big hit. I'd barely open a box before the employees were swarming to get them.

"Score! This is awesome!" they'd exclaim, eagerly grabbing a shirt. "Can I take another for my girlfriend?"

I also offered them to loyal customers at market. Years later, even after I'd sold the company, people told me they were wearing their T-shirts and how much they enjoyed them.

The *double entendre* was rarely lost. The only person who ever asked about it was my mother. "By the way," she said on the phone one day, 'I've been meaning to ask you. Why is it when people read the back of my Fiona's T-shirt, they start laughing?" I dutifully explained the other meaning.

"Ah!" she replied. "That's quite clever! Well, I shall continue to wear it with pride."

Natalie, slightly particular about her wardrobe, requested a shirt without the tagline. "No words, Mommy" she told me. "I just want flowers on my shirt." That was fortunate. She was only five, and I certainly didn't want to give the impression that my daughter walked around "baked," especially since I was a single mom running a business in Boulder.

*   *   *

Product creation kept me busy, and sometimes I got carried away with the possibilities. Offering a wide variety was important to me, as was considering people's allergies and other health issues. I was interested in offering a unique product line with choices that customers couldn't find elsewhere. Before long, I had created thirteen varieties of granola.

Producing them all was a challenge, since each required different ingredients, labels, and nutrition panels. There was limited space at the bakery, especially as sales increased. In addition, the more varieties, the higher the chance for errors with baking and packaging.

I took advantage of the errors by touting them at market as "limited edition" granolas— "Get them while you can!" Orange Walnut, Cinnamon Almond Coconut, Ginger Almond, Cranberry Walnut, and others filled my farmers market table whenever my bakers or packagers accidentally mixed together erroneous ingredients. If they tasted good, I sold them.

We also produced exclusive varieties at the request of individual restaurants, cafes, and food co-ops. For one local restaurant, I created Orange Cranberry. For a chain of breakfast and lunch cafes, we made Cinnamon Almond Raisin. For a co-op in Nederland, a nearby mountain town, I developed "Ned Head." I enjoyed creating these custom varieties, and the accounts were appreciative of the special attention and ability to offer their customers an exclusive mix.

My father got frustrated adding so many varieties to the spreadsheets. He kept up with the pricing for each new product, but as the list grew longer, his patience grew shorter. It became necessary to pare down the offerings. I said good-bye to Almond Raisin, Walnut Raisin, Nutty Raisin, Mixed Nut, Mixed Nut 'N Fruit, Cranberry Nut, Pecan, Tropical, Tropical Almond, and Papaya Walnut.

~5~
WHOLE FOODS: THE SERENDIPITY AISLE

"Knowledge speaks but wisdom listens."
—Jimi Hendrix
(Quote on boxes of Cinnamon Almond Granola)

Finding another place to bake became top priority. At the catering facility, it was only a matter of time before someone got hurt. Schlepping those heavy bags of ingredients and finished product up and down the stairs was only asking for trouble. I had already lost entire bins of granola because someone tripped on a step. I didn't want to risk more lost product or something even worse, like a serious injury.

The search began. I inquired with local bakeries, catering companies, and with my suppliers and Jill, since they called on numerous production facilities. These efforts came up blank. One day at market, my luck changed. I was chatting with Howard, a fellow vendor who produced a variety of baked goods. He was friendly and cheerful, and we had established a nice rapport. I asked him about his bakery, and if he happened to have space to rent. He thought a moment and said, "Actually, I guess I do. My last renter moved out a few weeks ago, and the other one comes in just once a month. The bakery's in South Boulder. If the location works for you, come on over and check it out."

South Boulder! That was music to my ears. By this time, Natalie was enrolled in school there, as her dad and I had moved to Boulder some months earlier. The proximity would facilitate the visits I often snuck in with Natalie on the days I didn't have her. I'd show up during one of her classes, usually art or music or P.E., or during her after-school program when she was on the playground or in the gym. She enjoyed my surprise visits, and I got in my "Natalie fix."

Howard's bakery was small but adequate, practically a stone's throw from Natalie's school, and cost only a little more than I'd been paying. He did his baking during the day, so the nights were mine. He had a rotating oven, something I'd never seen before, with five shelves, each able to accommodate six large baking pans. Being able to bake thirty pans of granola at once—compared with ten at the catering facility—was a huge difference. I would miss the interactions I'd had with the dumpling sisters and the flax cracker guys, especially those Friday nights when we were all there preparing for the next day's farmers market. But I knew I would also enjoy interacting with Howard. He was fun and talkative, played upbeat music, and was good-humored in his work and with his employees. I respected him from the get-go. He was honest, helpful, didn't mince words, and worked hard. Howard became a friend and mentor, and someone I could trust.

My employees at the catering facility found work with another company there, and replacing them was easy. Following Howard's advice, I posted the positions on the student employment website at the nearby University of Colorado. The response was astounding. What college kid wouldn't want to bake granola in Boulder, a town famous for its hippies and throwback-to-the-'60s culture?

I paid well—on average $3 to $5 more per hour than minimum wage—so most employees stayed with me for years. To me, the generous pay was worth it. In addition to increased loyalty and decreased turnover, the longer they stayed, the better workers they became. I also allowed them to purchase the granola wholesale.

My employees were cross-trained to bake and package. I paid them by the batch, based on what could reasonably be done in an hour of working diligently but not rushing. Usually, they made $13 to $15 an hour. Not bad for college students who worked with no supervision, played their own music, and had flexible hours as long as they were done and gone by the time Howard got there.

I'd made clear that pay would be docked if the granola or packaging didn't turn out as it should. But this rarely happened; if procedures were followed, it was a win-win situation. Most of my crew were gems:

hard working, efficient, punctual, and reliable. They normally worked in pairs and established a good rhythm. Since they often had class the next day and needed sleep and study time, they baked or packaged, cleaned up, and left.

Still, they could be sneaky. One day, Howard said to me, "Fiona, the bottom of the oven is covered with granola. Your bakers must be stirring the granola with the pans still on the shelves."

"Oh, no!" I replied. "I'm sure they wouldn't do *that*. I've told them to carry the pans to the table to stir."

"Well, it's the only thing I can figure that's causing so much granola to spill into the oven," he said. I looked inside and saw the floor completely covered in granola.

"Oh dear," I thought. Not only was this a health hazard, but it was also lost product. I confronted my bakers. "Are you guys stirring the granola while it's sitting on the oven shelves?"

"Oh, no!" came the reply. "We wouldn't do *that!*"

"Okay, then how do you explain all the granola on the oven floor?"

"Maybe there's spillage when we pull the pans in and out of the oven," they suggested.

That didn't make sense. When the granola first goes in the oven, it's heavy and sticky. There's no way it would escape from the pan. As it bakes, it becomes lighter and loses the stickiness. I could envision a little granola escaping in transport after the last stir, but the pans had high walls, so I couldn't picture much getting out.

"Well," I told them, "you'd better not be stirring it in the oven. That kind of shortcut is unacceptable. You simply must take the time to carry the pans to the table first." I told them to sweep up the oven floor, which was no small task. The side access door was tiny, and an average-sized adult had difficulty climbing through, much less maneuvering inside. After sweeping up such a mess, I figured, surely they'd be more careful.

The problem seemed solved—until Howard told me again a couple of months later that the oven floor was covered in granola.

"What!" I exclaimed. "My bakers insisted they aren't stirring the granola while it's on the oven shelves."

"Well," he said, "someone needs to clean it up, and it's not going to be me. If it continues, I'm afraid you'll have to replace your bakers. Stirring the granola on the shelves is the only way this could happen."

This time, I cleaned the oven myself—not happily, but I climbed in and did it. The problem needed to be solved. I decided the only thing to do was walk in one night and hope it was during a stir. There were two in every baking shift.

I knew what time they started, approximately how long it took to mix the ingredients and fill the pans, and the baking time between stirs. I did my calculations, and walked into the bakery unannounced one night the following week.

Lo and behold, there they were—two bakers standing at the oven stirring the granola as it sat in pans on the oven shelves. I was furious.

"Just as Howard suspected!" I exclaimed. "You guys are *so* busted."

They'd been caught red-handed. "Are the others doing this too?" I asked.

"Yeah, we all do it."

"Well," I said, "it stops tonight, or you're all fired."

I hoped the threat would work. It did. There was no way for them to stir granola on the shelves without being caught, since the oven floor was too hot for them to clean the night they baked, and Howard arrived at 4 a.m.

I let him know he'd been right, and apologized on behalf of my bakers. He just smiled and thanked me for taking care of it.

Natalie loved going to the bakery after school. Books in tow, she'd climb onto the bags of oats or sesame seeds and read contentedly or do art projects while I loaded goods for deliveries, put ingredients away, check in with the packagers, and did other work. There were always goodies to eat, and she got lots of attention from whomever was at the bakery.

Howard said Natalie's visits reminded him of the days he and his wife had spent baking together, each with one of their daughters in a kiddie backpack. I appreciated his flexibility with my schedule as a single mom, and the chance to buy his baked goods at wholesale prices. Natalie loved his cinnamon rolls, and I loved the blueberry bran muffins.

Howard also helped with ingredient sourcing, since he knew far more suppliers than I did, and I met other food manufacturers at his bakery. Billy, for one, who made bagels the traditional way—boiling, not steaming, in a huge vat that used to be at the bakery. There was also a hemp ice cream cookie manufacturer and came in once a month, late at night. He made delicious ice cream cookies, and left some for everyone, which we all gobbled up.

Many of Howard's former renters joked that his bakery was their jumping off platform. Boulder Ice Cream had started there, as did a national pie company. I was one in a long stream of food entrepreneurs who shared his space, so it was a bit legendary to be there.

A couple months after moving into Howard's bakery, via a serendipitous meeting, my granola was accepted into Whole Foods. Earlier that summer, I had delivered a case of granola to the owner of a gift basket company. As I left, she said, "So, guess who lives next door?" I had no idea. She broke into a smile. "The general manager of Whole Foods."

"*Really?*" I asked. "That's cool." She asked if I had brought granola to the store for review. "No, I've been so busy, and I'm not sure I'm ready for Whole Foods."

"Well," she said, "the manager's name is Louis, and he's a really nice guy. Maybe you should leave a bag with me, and I'll give it to him. If he likes it, that might help you get in."

"Okay," I replied. "I guess it can't hurt." As I went to my car to grab a bag for her, a car pulled into the driveway. I wondered if the driver might be Louis, and took a chance.

"Hi!" I exclaimed, "Are you Louis?"

"Yeees," came the tentative reply. "Who are you?"

"I'm Fiona, and I've recently started a granola company. Would it be okay if I gave you a bag? Kathy told me you're the manager of Whole Foods. I'd love to get my product into the store."

"There's a very competitive approval process," he said.

"That's okay. I'd just like you to try the granola and let me know what you think." He hesitated.

"I happen to have a few bags in the car," I continued. "I'd love for you to try the Almond—it's our best seller."

"Okay. But there is no guarantee we can get it into the system."

"No worries!" I answered as I handed him the bag. "Maybe it's serendipity that we met."

"Perhaps," he replied.

The next day, Louis called. "Fiona, this granola is fantastic! My family went bonkers over it. How soon can you bring over four bags of each variety? They need to go to Austin for approval, but I think it will happen."

Louis said one of the grocery managers was going to Austin the next morning and could take the granola with him. I delivered it to Steve, the grocery manager, that evening. Perhaps the personal delivery expedited the process, because Whole Foods approved the granolas in what, I later learned, was record time.

Over the months, I established wonderful rapport with the employees there. Natalie and I spent so much time at the store, the only Whole Foods in Boulder, that we befriended receivers, stockers, cashiers, and people in the produce department. Six days a week, I was either checking inventory or restocking.

When I chatted with customers, they'd say, "Oh! Are *you* Fiona? I just love this granola! We eat it every day for breakfast." Or "Oh! I thought I recognized you from Farmers Market. You stock the shelves yourself?" Or "Could you make another granola without nuts? The only ones are Orange Crunch and Cinnamon Raisin; I don't like orange-flavored foods, and I don't like raisins."

Natalie and I soon became fixtures at the store. Whole Foods and the farmers market became my social life since, because of my hectic schedule, most of my pre-granola friendships had fallen by the wayside. My new acquaintances were customers, store employees, farmers, and other business owners. I missed my other friends but was grateful to have established these other enjoyable relationships.

For the most part, production ran smoothly. The challenges were part of the learning curve. One morning, the accountant at a local grocery called: "Fiona, you need to get over here right away."

"What's wrong?"

"The weight of your bags is what's wrong," she said, "and we're not happy about it."

I immediately jumped in the car and went over. When I walked in, my eyes met a large bin filled with my granola bags, which she had tossed in carelessly. I looked at her dumbfounded. "The Colorado Department of Weights and Measures stopped by today," she said. "They weighed your bags. Every one of them came up light."

I was in shock. "That can't be," I replied. "We put exactly twenty-four ounces in each. I'm very strict with my packagers to not underfill or overfill the bags. Something is just not right."

She wasn't in the mood to hear my explanation. "All I know is that these bags are light, and if a fine comes down, you'll be the one to pay. You can take these bags, because we can't sell them."

Distraught, I carted the granola home and called the woman from Weights and Measures. Surprisingly, she didn't seem upset. "I don't think you're trying to cheat your customers," she said. "The fact that the bags are all so close in weight is impressive. But they're all consistently underweight." The error wasn't egregious—a quarter-ounce to half-ounce, but it was enough to pull the bags.

"What kind of scale are you using?" she asked.

"A Pelouze," I replied. She learned it was not digital.

"Well, that's your problem! Unless it's digital, no wonder your weights are off. Those other scales are notorious for being inaccurate. Go get yourself a digital scale, and I think that will solve the problem. We'll let the infraction go this time. I trust that if your bags are weighed in future, they won't come up light again." I thanked her and assured her I would take care of it.

When I explained what had happened to the store accountant, she was much friendlier. "I really didn't think you were trying to cheat anyone, Fiona. The whole scenario just caught us by surprise, and we don't like shelves to be empty."

Turns out, the Weights and Measures woman had found other companies out of compliance that day. Somehow, that eased the blow.

~6~
A BAR IS BORN

"It takes courage to grow up and become who you really are."

—e. e. cummings

Since I had been making granola for over twenty years before going into business, developing new varieties was easy. The cereals were well-received and selling beyond my wildest dreams; my customers had become loyal patrons. I was satisfied with the offerings, and the one product line kept me very busy.

At the start of my second year at farmers market, customers started asking for new products.

"Can you please develop a granola bar? You make the best granola on the planet, so I can only imagine how good your bars would be!"

"I've tried to turn your granola into bars and couldn't figure it out. But, I'm sure you can!"

"There aren't any good energy bars out there. Certainly it wouldn't be too difficult for you to create one!"

The continuing compliments my granola received boosted my confidence. Eventually I conceded. Maybe they were right: How hard could it be?

Granola bars were not a staple of my diet. Most were very sweet, contained preservatives and fillers, and left a strange aftertaste. Many of them were no healthier than a candy bar. I decided I would create a granola bar better than any other—healthy, not overly sweet, with interesting flavor combinations and a chewy texture. A new challenge in front of me, I set to work.

Although it seemed logical to use the granola I already made, that didn't work. I experimented with various syrups, but none would bind the crispy cereal together. I realized the bars would have to be their own creation, starting from scratch.

I mixed my ingredients together: various combinations of nuts, seeds, chocolate chips, dried fruit, and nut butters, all in a base of oats. Although some of the results were flavorful, none resulted in what one could call a granola bar. They either crumbled or were sticky and not easy to cut.

At the time, I was participating in a Life Writing workshop at a local bookstore. Although there had been twenty people on the waiting list when I signed up, the instructor had allowed me in. "I considered what each person hoped to get out of the class," he said. "For some reason, I believe you're supposed to be in the group."

It was a workshop in which our essays and short stories—often containing personal and delicate subject matter—allowed us considerable opportunity to bond, form friendships, and establish trust. Many tears were shed during those eight weeks as we bared our souls.

Each week, I brought in my latest granola bar creation. Although most of my classmates' comments were positive, no one *loved* the bars. One night after class, as we sat around munching and commenting on what we liked and didn't like about the latest revision, one woman piped up. "You know, Fiona, I could help you with these bars. I own a cooking school and have experience with product development."

"You *own* a cooking school? And you're just telling me that *now*? Yes, I would love help developing these bars!" Thus began my professional relationship with Joanne.

I learned that she was a master chef, with countless ideas for product creation. We discussed ingredients, flavor combinations, and textures, agreeing on four dense and chewy varieties. I had utmost confidence that if anyone could help me create a superior granola bar, it was Joanne.

The next week, she called. "Your bars are ready!" she happily exclaimed.

"So soon?" I asked. I'd spent the better part of three months doing bar development, and Joanne had spent less than a week. The following day, I went to her house. The bars were heavenly. Chewy and dense, fresh and flavorful. The sweetness level was perfect. After I told her how amazing they were, she explained the recipes. I learned that at her school, she always used the healthiest ingredients available, no matter the price or difficulty in obtaining them.

Some of the ingredients weren't feasible for me. For instance, the bars contained walnut oil. Not only are walnuts a common allergen, but the oil was very expensive. It also had to be refrigerated, space I didn't have at Howard's bakery.

Two of the varieties contained Turkish apricots with no sulfites, which Joanne had chopped by hand. They added moisture, flavor, and texture to the bars, but they were sticky and hard, which made cutting difficult. And they cost a third more than apricots that had the preservative.

I was hesitant, but Joanne made it sound easy. "Just get yourself a really sharp knife, and you'll see what a breeze it is!"

Against my better judgment, I ordered twenty-five pounds, the only bulk size available. Those apricots were a nightmare, bonding to the knife and gumming up a food processor; by the end of our first production run, I realized they needed to go. We had only used two pounds of apricots—what to do with the remaining twenty-three? Give them to hungry college students, of course.

Joanne's method with my bars was to make everything from scratch, as she did in her cooking school. To begin, she ground the nut butters herself. "It's super-easy," she assured me, "and it will save you money over buying pre-ground." By that point, I was starting to doubt Joanne's "super-easy" claims.

To grind the nuts, she had used a powerful food processor called a Robot Coupe, which cost $1,000 to $2,000. I bought a less expensive, but good-quality, processor instead, thinking it would suffice. It didn't. The time we spent making nut butter doubled the cost of the product, because of labor.

I decided to purchase preground nut butters, which were only available using roasted nuts. That did not make Joanne happy. She favored use of raw ingredients whenever possible, mostly because they're more easily absorbed into the body. Health attributes aside, I preferred the roasted over the raw. They were more flavorful, and they gave the bars a deeper color and more character.

Joanne's recipes called for ground flax seeds, which she suggested we grind ourselves. With this ingredient, her suggestion made sense. Using a basic coffee grinder, the seeds were easy and fast to grind. With no refrigeration at Howard's bakery, I didn't want to risk pre-ground seeds turning rancid, which they do if not refrigerated.

Joanne had created the bars using golden flax seeds, which were almost twice as expensive as brown. The golden, she said, "are much more attractive and will lend a lighter color to the bars." I wasn't concerned with color tone variation, so I ordered brown.

To flavor one of the bars, Joanne incorporated espresso syrup imported from France. I suggested using real espresso, but she was adamant about the French syrup. Delicious, yes—and expensive. I agreed, mostly to keep our relationship healthy—her patience was wearing thin because of the many ingredients changes. When my supplier stopped carrying it a few years later, we simply brewed strong coffee as a replacement, with a result almost identical to what the expensive syrup gave us.

Papaya stayed, although I bought it diced rather than chop the spears ourselves as Joanne had suggested. Grated ginger also remained, although at first I'd resisted using it. First, without refrigeration, it turns moldy—which I learned upon throwing away almost thirty pounds of it. Instead of buying wholesale quantities, I headed to the Asian grocery store before each production run and bought just enough for each batch.

Second, the ginger involved washing, peeling, and grating. One day, Joanne casually mentioned that she didn't peel the ginger before shredding it.

"You don't peel the ginger?" I asked in amazement. I was sure the peel would be tough and unappetizing.

"The first bars I made had the peel in them," she assured me. "You couldn't even tell."

Although we had our disagreements, I trusted Joanne's culinary expertise. The next time we made the bars, I told my baker to leave the skin on.

"Leave the skin on?" he asked. "Okay, whatever you say. At least I won't have to spend all that time cutting it off!"

With a bit of trepidation, we tried the finished product. It was fantastic! And Joanne was right: I couldn't tell the difference. Leaving the skin on saved both labor and ingredient costs, since we didn't peel off approximately 10 percent of the ginger. It also lowered the risk of my baker injuring himself with a sharp knife.

We had developed four varieties of energy bars. For the first, we settled on a name immediately: Chocolate Chip Peanut Butter. Not a lot more to be said. It was practical and straightforward, and we hoped it would appeal to anyone who liked that ingredient combination.

Naming the others was enjoyable but came with its challenges. Joanne suggested Tropical Heat Wave. I had to give her credit for the creativity but didn't find it suitable for an energy bar. To me, the name evoked island dwellers caught in an intense heat spell, which left them limp and apathetic—not a good vision for an energy bar.

Joanne had also suggested Piña Colada. That didn't work—because of its sugary taste and unsteady supply, I had taken out the pineapple from her original recipe. I liked the word "tropical" because even without the pineapple, they featured two tropical ingredients: papaya and coconut. I called those bars Tropical Spice. Although I loved the name, the word "spice" may have discouraged people from trying it over the years.

Our brainstorming sessions were fun, but they created a bit of tension. The morning I shared my lack of enthusiasm for Tropical Heat Wave, Joanne said, "Well, you're really gonna love the name of the next bar." I took a deep breath as she exclaimed, "Mocha Express-Oh!" With the exclamation mark. I pondered the name.

The bar had caffeine, which was important to convey. It was chocolate-based, contained that expensive French coffee syrup, and also had both cocoa powder and chocolate chips, so it was packed with ingredients to perk up anyone. Although the name was cute and imaginative, I felt customers might think we'd misspelled "espresso" and meant to say "Mocha Espress-Oh!" There was also no need for the word "espresso" if we were saying "mocha." I told her I'd think about it.

Since the start of my business, I had found walks, hikes, and bike rides the perfect times to solve whatever snags came up. Somehow, my brain relaxed and ideas flowed more easily than when I was sitting at my desk. For the next few days, during my walks and bike rides, I thought about that bar.

Fun names appealed to me as long as the "fun" was descriptive and not too goofy. Out walking one sunny day, "Magical Mocha" popped into my head. I stopped in my tracks. "Magical Mocha!" I exclaimed out loud. "I love it!"

I've always been a fan of alliteration, and the word "magical" conveyed a bit of mystery. The stoners might hope for a special ingredient, since the bars were quite brownie-like. Others might wonder what was so magical about them. Those bars were rich and dreamy and chocolaty, and to me, they *were* magical. I ran the name by Joanne. Although she still preferred "Mocha Express-Oh!" she agreed that I'd found a good name.

The fourth bar featured orange oil and cranberries, two flavors we hadn't seen combined in an energy bar. Moist and fruity, it was addictive. Figuring out a creative name proved difficult for both of us, so we kept it simple: Cranberry Orange.

Names and recipes complete, my next project was pricing. Who else to turn to but my father? In addition to his doctorate in physics, he'd gotten an MBA as a fallback when science funding hit hard times and there was concern the solar observatory where he worked would be shut down. Always doing his best to provide for his family, he saw value in obtaining a business degree; it would be a good fallback if he eventually needed to pursue work outside of science. The added degree was a good fit considering his love of numbers and mathematical equations.

I believed the MBA meant he understood the intricacies of profit margins, balance sheets, cash flow, profit and loss statements, gross vs. net, cash vs. accrual, and other aspects of accounting. Only later would I realize that was not the case. He had gotten the degree through a correspondence course some twenty years earlier, before the advent of online courses. Excel spreadsheets and accounting programs like QuickBooks hadn't been invented yet. Nonetheless, he understood math better than I did, was retired, and agreed to help me—at no charge.

Working on numbers for my granola, he helped figure the costs and calculate wholesale and retail pricing. The data for each flavor had its own spreadsheet, which helped keep track of changing ingredient prices. His calculations seemed thorough and logical, incorporating rent, labor, ingredients, insurance, packaging, mileage, phone, internet, utilities, certifications, advertising, legal fees, shipping costs, graphic design, dues and subscriptions, linen service, office and kitchen supplies, licenses, repairs, maintenance, tax preparation, travel, commissions, delivery fees, and lost profit due to water evaporation during baking.

My father spent countless hours on those spreadsheets. I think he enjoyed the challenge. Except for his stock market hobby, he didn't have many projects that included analyzing numbers. The spreadsheets, I told myself, helped keep his mind sharp and contributed to one of his favorite pastimes. I didn't question his accuracy with the numbers.

When the time came to price the bars, I called him. "Hi, Dad! I have a new project for you."

"Yeees?" came the tentative reply. I told him about the bars. After a bit of hesitation, he agreed to create spreadsheets. I sent him data, he input the numbers, and *voila!*—I had my pricing. Through the years, he repeated the process for each new item I created. At one point, I suggested he patent his software and market the program to budding entrepreneurs. He laughed, saying the spreadsheets weren't refined and were somewhat unorthodox. Only later did I learn how true that was.

Rolling out the bar dough was no easy task. It was heavy, dense, and sticky—work that, my bakers said, built their muscles. The shorter ones stood on a pallet to gain height for the necessary downward pressure. That wasn't adequate for me, as I didn't have the strength to roll them from a standing position. I climbed onto the counter and leaned right over the sheet tray, funneling my ninety pounds down through my arms and into that rolling pin.

Howard had generously offered his sheeter, a machine designed to flatten dough to a desired thickness. Unfortunately, the process backfired: instead of forming the dough into a neat slab, the sheeter spat it in all directions, splattering Howard's bakery with chunks of sticky dough.

Buying equipment like the extruders that large energy bar manufacturers use or utensils specifically made for scoring and cutting
would have been very expensive. I had already invested in new packaging, design of the granola bar logo, an expensive rolling pin, high-
quality storage containers, and hours of training to teach employees
the baking and packaging process. I had also paid Joanne a hefty sum
for product development.

Although our bars were noticeably homemade, the goal was for
them to resemble the size and shape of mainstream energy bars. This
required a uniform look. To size them consistently, we first removed
the edges, then cut them using a five-wheel pastry cutter. Although
we could adjust the space between the wheels, they didn't hold in
place very well, resulting in inconsistent sizes, shapes, and weights.

There was a welding shop that had been in Boulder for decades,
and per Howard's suggestion, I popped in one day and shared our
predicament with the owner. He looked at the utensil for a bit and
said no one had ever asked him to weld a pastry cutter. "But," he said,
"I can give it a go."

When I returned the following week, he said, "I think you'll be
happy. Seems to be sturdy, and those wheels won't be moving. I added
a space bar to make the apparatus more durable. This should last quite
a while, young lady." I smiled, thanked him and paid the fee, and offered him a granola bar. He was right. That pastry cutter never broke,
and the wheels held their spacing and orientation, even after cutting
thousands of energy bars.

My bakers enjoyed the bar edges straight from the oven. Warm and
chewy, they were heavenly. They made great snacks for Natalie's
lunches; she usually chose Chocolate Chip Peanut Butter, but sometimes she wanted Cranberry Orange. She shared them liberally with
her friends. "My daughter just loves those granola bars Natalie brings
to school! Where can I buy them?" parents asked. Or, "My son raves
about the granola bars Natalie brings in. Do you make those?"

I also brought them to market to offer samples. Customers took
one bite and exclaimed, "Wow! That is the best energy bar I've ever
eaten! Do you sell these in the stores?" Many customers, including

professional athletes, stopped by market just to buy the bars. One woman thanked me for making them and said she brought them to work every day because, "They don't raise my blood sugar the way other bars do." During the months market was closed, I kept bar edges in the car and handed them to people on the street corners.

For the bars' nutritional analysis, I was eager to find a less expensive option than the $500 I'd paid for the granola analysis. Through other food entrepreneurs, I learned about the College of Health and Human Sciences at Colorado State University in Fort Collins. Ahuva, a Ph.D. student there, ran food nutritionals for a fraction of the price. She was Israeli and spoke with a lively accent.

As part of her dissertation work on the benefits of Omega-3 fatty acids, she was developing an energy bar made with fish oil. When she learned about my bars, she was intrigued and agreed to run the analysis.

She loved my samples when I brought them to her the following week, and she let me try her creation. She used an eclectic array of ingredients, and the end result was amazing. The fish oil was undetectable because of the base of dark chocolate, butter, and cinnamon. She gave me a slew of bars, and Natalie and I gobbled them up.

After the analysis was complete, we stayed in touch. I attended Ahuva's dissertation defense and encouraged her to market the energy bar. She didn't want to be bothered and suggested I include it in my line. I liked the idea but already had enough to handle. The fish oil and butter would need refrigeration, and the other ingredients required shelf space that wasn't available. Unfortunately, Ahuva's bar never made it to market. It was outstanding, in its taste and texture profiles and in its health benefits as well.

The tagline "Organic Goodness in Every Bite!" was appropriate for both the granola and the bars, but the "I'm Perfectly Baked!" tagline was more granola-specific. A slogan just for the bars might help distinguish them.

To create a second tagline, I went off on a bike ride.

"Granola Bar Meets Energy Bar" popped into my head in the first half-hour. "That's it!" I thought. Since they were chewy like an energy bar but mostly comprised of oats, they were a combination. When I got home, I created the labels: the logo, weight, variety, and two taglines on the front, and the nutritional information on the back.

One summer, I was invited to participate in Boulder's annual Jewish festival. It fell on a Sunday when Natalie wasn't with me. Never one to decline marketing opportunities or a chance to gain new customers, I accepted. The day was hot and the flow of people nonstop; I took only a few minutes' break the entire day. Afterward, I quickly broke down my booth, ready to go home and have a cold beer.

Just as I was about to leave, a man appeared and asked, "You got any granola bars left?" He had bought a Chocolate Chip Peanut Butter bar earlier that afternoon.

"Oh," I sighed. "I'm sure I do, but I've already packed up the boxes and was about to leave. Would you mind coming by market next Saturday and buying some then?"

He said he was leaving for Mexico the next day and wanted to take the bars with him. "I have a sensitive stomach," he explained, "and I want to bring snacks that are easy on my system. I'll be there a few weeks." I asked how many he wanted. "How about twenty-five?" he replied. "Would that make it worth your while to unpack the box?"

"Oh, it most certainly would!" I dug out two caddies of Chocolate Chip Peanut Butter bars. "Each caddy holds fifteen bars," I explained. "Would you be okay with two full caddies and buy thirty instead?"

"Absolutely," he replied.

A few months later, he appeared again at farmers market. With him was his new girlfriend, whom he'd met online but had gone to Mexico to meet in person. "I had to bring her here," he said. "She fell in love with those bars, so I told her we'd visit the market so she could meet you." The two of them joined my Spanish group, and we've stayed friends ever since.

Finally, after a long, costly, and at times frustrating process, the bars were ready to present to the stores. They were selling well on my website, at farmers market, and through gift basket companies, athletic clubs, and coffee shops. The display cases, or "caddies," were simple white boxes that we folded together and sealed using the top flap.

The Valentine's Day after creating the Magical Mocha bars, I decided to thank my accounts for their continued support. My great aunt had gifted me with cookie cutters in the shape of hearts. I suggested to Natalie that we cut a few trays of mocha bars into hearts and pass them out for Valentine's Day. She loved the idea. I asked my bakers to produce extra bars during the next production run, and I brought the trays home so Natalie and I could cut them together. We chose two sizes of hearts, and packed one of each into little clear bags. We printed out pink cards, punched a hole in them, and attached them to the bags with a red twist-tie that we used to seal the package. The outside of the card showed our logo. The inside read, "Thank you for your continued support and encouragement! Happy Valentine's Day!" We each signed our names. Natalie went with me to distribute the chocolate hearts to our accounts. They were well received.

*   *   *

One of my favorite members of the grocery "team" (Whole Foods' term for its employees) was Spice. He was a jolly fellow, good-natured, and supportive of my endeavors. When I first got my granola into the store, he ordered and managed inventory in the grocery department. We sometimes chatted while I did my deliveries. He often said, "Fiona, you need to get your granola into distribution. The time you spend doing these deliveries could be spent on sales and marketing and developing new products. At least find yourself a delivery person." I appreciated his interest and told him that I might do that someday.

Spice moved into the receiving department, which is where I found him when I brought in the packaged energy bars, ready for the stores. He had tried samples during product development but hadn't seen the finished product. He broke into a smile. "Way to go, Fiona. The packaging is pretty home-grown, but it's good enough for now. What's the wholesale price?"

I shared the price my dad had suggested—higher than almost every other bar on the market—and told him I was inclined to bring it down. He replied, "Make some money, Fiona! You know we're gonna make our margin, and you need to make yours. Isn't that why you're in business?" I realized he was right.

"Your granola is the highest priced in the store," he said, "and look how well it's selling. People are willing to pay more for a high-quality product. You've established a following, and I think customers will buy the bars." I trusted his instincts. "Okay," I sighed. "Let's just hope they sell."

Not only had I gone to Whole Foods that day to show Spice the finished product but I also had brought extras for other team members. Get the grocery folks hooked on a product, I'd learned, and they'll recommend it to customers. "Do you have a spare caddy of each variety?" Spice asked.

"Yes," I replied. "I planned to pass them out to team members."

"Well, if you can spare a caddy of each, I'll get them into the system right now, and we can put them on the shelf." I was in shock.

Although the authorization for my granola had been quick and easy, I was prepared for a longer approval process for the bars, and to send them to regional headquarters in Austin. "This is simply a line extension," he said. "You're a vendor in our system, so you've already been approved. I can probably get these in today."

"Wow! That would be fantastic! Thank you so much!" I handed him a caddy of each variety.

That night, I shared the story with Natalie. I related how helpful Spice had been and what a huge favor he had done for us. She listened, processing the information. Then she got up, found paper and pencil, and started drawing. She folded the paper into fourths. At the top of the page, she drew a granola bar. Then she wrote:

> Thank you! Spise. For being so nise!
> We aprishrat that you'v ben so kind to us.
> Why do you have so meny peersings?
>   Love Natalie

True enough, Spice had piercings. His ears had gauges, those large earrings that stretch the earlobe and need to be replaced as the hole enlarges. His nose was pierced, and he sported a few tattoos. Natalie was keenly observant, and she didn't let those aspects pass her by.

She opened the card and drew Spice, with his piercings, then wrote "Spise" with an arrow pointing to him. She drew a wide smile, with mouth open, and a dialogue bubble: "I Love Fionas prodect." On the adjacent page, she drew shelves of granola, granola bar caddies, and signs that read, "Fionas." On the back, she drew a heart with curlicues at the bottom and wrote "I Love you Spise" inside it. At the top, she added, "This page is dron by Fiona."

"Honey," I said, "I didn't draw that page, and maybe we shouldn't tell Spice that I love him." She just smiled and said, "Let's give it to him the next time we go in."

I gave her a big hug, thanked her for making the card, and said okay. How could I refuse? He'd get a kick out of it, and I wanted to honor Natalie's efforts to make him such a heartfelt gift. A few days later, Natalie gave him the card. He broke into a huge smile. "This is friggin' fantastic! Thank you, Natalie! I'm gonna hang it right here so everyone can enjoy it."

Sure enough, he did. For well over a year, Natalie's card hung in that office for all to see. Occasionally, receivers would ask, "Fiona, did your daughter make that for Spice?"

"Yep," I'd proudly reply. "That's my Natalie."

~7~

TALE OF A TOOTH

"We see in the world what we carry in our hearts."

—Anonymous

(Quote on caddies of Almond Chocolate Chip Quinoa Bars)

The positive work environment I had established was based on two principles: Treat employees well and pay a fair wage. Turnover was costly. I also didn't want Howard worrying about a slew of C.U. students gaining access to his bakery.

All in all, production went well. The workers were efficient, enjoyed their jobs, and turned out wonderful products. Though all were cross-trained, they didn't get routine practice in each—the baking suffered when the packagers had that job, and vice versa.

I found that, when packaging, the women paid closer attention to detail than their male counterparts—and there were a lot of details. The men would sometimes use too much force, creasing both bags and labels, and wrinkling the filled bags as they put them on the shelves.

In the case of two stoners among the packagers, my patience ran thin. I call these guys "stoners" for good reason—I never saw them straight. Their droopy red eyes and mellow attitude didn't bother me. What did was that they took *forever* to package. They were so slow that their pay came out on average at 5 cents per unit, whereas most of the others earned 20 cents. When I pointed this out, they smiled and said it was fine. They enjoyed the work, and the hours were great for their school schedule. I told them I knew about their stoner ways but that since the scent was undetectable, their habits were not harming the product. Still, I warned that if they were ever caught smoking there, they would be fired. They assured me that would never happen, and as far as I know, it never did. When they eventually moved on, I was a little sad. They weren't efficient, but they were friendly, fun, and could always bring a smile to my face.

In time, business grew to the point that I needed an assistant to help with deliveries, orders, scheduling, administration, and other tasks. I placed an ad on Craigslist and hired a woman named Isis. She was my age, had managed a retail clothing shop, and would work the night hours we had access to the bakery.

One day, I contacted the manager at a local art cinema. He was keen to support local artists, products, and vendors. After discussing snack options, he asked if I could create granola clusters, similar in size to popcorn, that were clumpy, easy to eat by hand, and slightly tacky. Always eager for the next challenge, I told him I'd see what I could do.

Agave, as much as I loved it as a sweetener, was not a good clumping agent. I settled on brown rice syrup instead. I had discovered how thick and sticky it was when we used it as a sweetener during an agave shortage.

That had been no fun. I had called Madhava, our distributor, to place an order, only to learn that the farmers in Mexico were having crop problems which had dried up the supply. "We have no idea when we'll have more," the sales agent said, "but we can sell you honey in the interim, so just let us know."

My search for a new sweetener began. Barley malt extract yielded dark granola that wasn't sweet enough, and the brown rice syrup caused the granola to clump too much. Luckily, I discovered chicory root syrup, which one of my suppliers had started importing from Belgium. It was a good replacement—thin, light in color, with a low-glycemic index and neutral flavor. But after a couple of months, that became unavailable as well. We had no choice but to use honey. When I called Madhava to order it, though, good news came across the line. "Guess what, Fiona? We just got in a new supply of agave! The crop issues have been resolved, and we don't expect the supply to run out again. Would you like some?" I let out a huge sigh of relief. "Indeed!" I replied.

Shortly before my conversation with Roy, the theater manager, I had discontinued my Trail Mix granola. It contained peanuts, raisins, and

SunDrops, a healthy alternative to M&Ms. SunDrops are delicious but cost four times the price of M&Ms. Although the Trail Mix sold well at farmers market and on my website, the SunDrops were cutting too deeply into the profit margin.

Since we had a fair amount of SunDrops on hand, I saw the clusters as a good way to polish them off. They would bump up the price, but theater snacks command top dollar, and I felt moviegoers would pay for a local product unique to that cinema. If the clusters sold, I could always buy more SunDrops.

Creating the clusters wasn't difficult. I took the Trail Mix granola recipe, replaced the agave with brown rice syrup, and skipped the stirs during the baking process. The granola baked into a solid mass. After it cooled, we broke it into chunks by hand. The process was a sticky affair, both in mixing and cleaning, but the result was delicious. Roy was thrilled, as were customers. "Fiona!" they'd exclaim, "I went to the movies last night and tried your granola clusters. They're so good, and they're a great alternative to popcorn!" They became a popular item at the cinema, and we baked them on a regular basis.

Roy called one Wednesday to request six cases of Trail Mix for a big event that would take place two days later. We'd have to double up production, and because my bakers' schedules prevented them from adding a shift, Isis and I would jump in, working together into the wee hours of the morning.

Normally, I wouldn't have minded. Sleep deprivation had become the norm, so another short night was no big deal. What bothered me was that I ran the risk of missing a momentous event. Natalie was five, and her first tooth—a front upper one—was about to fall out. Since she was scheduled to be at my house, I'd probably get to see it. But, what was I to do? I had promised Roy those clusters.

Natalie's dad agreed to take her an extra night. I chose to keep her Wednesday, in hopes it would come out. Since she enjoyed playing with her tooth, I encouraged her to wiggle it even more. "Maybe it will fall out, honey! Won't that be exciting?" She wiggled and wiggled, but it was simply not ready.

Dismayed and discouraged, I brought her to school the next morning. "I'll miss you so much tonight, honey," I told her, "and I'll be thinking about you when I'm in the bakery."

"I know, Mommy," she replied. "I'll try to keep my tooth in there till I see you again!" She knew how important this was for me and wanted to allow me that indulgence.

That night in the bakery, I knew. I just *knew*. Her tooth would fall out, and I would miss it. And all to bake granola clusters for the cinema. I was on the verge of tears all night, and Isis detected my grief. "What's going on, Fiona?" she asked. "You never act this way." I told her about the tooth, and she tried to console me.

We didn't leave the bakery until 3 a.m. It had been a long night filled with anguished thoughts. Through the dark hours, a distressed voice tormented me: "Remember why you started this company, Fiona." I had done it to have flexible hours and more time with Natalie. Missing out on milestones was not in the equation.

I called her dad the next morning. "Did her tooth fall out?" I asked.

"Yeah," he replied, "it did." My heart sank. I thanked him for taking her and hung up. Then I broke into uncontrollable sobs. Through the angry tears, I made a pact with myself to not let it happen again. I would either find a way to not compromise our time together or simply not make the kind of promise I had.

When I picked Natalie up from school, she broke into a huge smile and presented me with her tooth. "I told Daddy you would want to see it," she said. She showed off her gap, and I gave her a big hug. Then she noticed my sadness. "What's wrong, Mommy? Aren't you happy my tooth fell out?"

I told her I was just sorry to have missed it. And that if I hadn't made those granola clusters, I would have been the one to see it come out. She looked at me intently. "That's okay. I'll make sure you see the next one fall out!"

Natalie was proud of her missing tooth, and she brought it to farmers market the next day. "Oh! You lost your first tooth!" customers exclaimed. "That's so exciting!" She smiled, showing off her gap, basking in the attention. I, on the other hand, felt like a deflated balloon. I convinced myself I was a lousy mom who had majorly screwed up her priorities. But I was happy for Natalie, and it was fun to be with her as she showed off her big accomplishment.

As it turns out, Natalie was right—I did see the next tooth fall out. And the one after that. Witnessing the loss of second and third teeth can never match that first one. I had endured a hard lesson. Life's lessons *are* hard sometimes, and certainly for me, that was one of the most painful.

~8~

Refreshing the Lotus Flowers

"The measure of who we are is what we do with what we have."

—Anonymous

I was in Brad's office one morning working on the website. "So Fiona," he casually asked, "are you happy with your logo?"

"Of course!" I replied. "I'm very happy with my logo."

"Well, I like it too, but I have to say, those digital flowers have always bothered me. I think we could drastically improve your logo if we freshen up those lotus flowers." His point was well taken—those digital flowers didn't do justice to my brand, and they were not what one would call stylish. He suggested I call an artist friend of his. To update my logo with a fresh look seemed worth the few hundred dollars she would charge.

When Angela called the following week, I rushed over to see the new look. Upon laying my eyes on the watercolor, I started to cry. What she had done to transform the flowers and lily pads was nothing short of amazing. The beauty swept me away, and my emotions along with it. I gave her a huge hug and told her how grateful I was. She seemed surprised at my emotion but was delighted I liked the new version so much.

Brad was equally pleased. "Wow, Fiona, this is gonna do wonders!" He scanned her painting into my logo, and *presto!* The look was sophisticated and artistic. I was proud of my new image, and pleased I had taken Brad's advice.

My third year at farmers market, the gluten-free craze surfaced. I was losing a good number of customers because I had no gluten-free granola. Gluten-free oats were not available, and other gluten-free grains couldn't easily be flaked. Not knowing what to do, I called Joanne.

A few days later, she had an answer: "How about creating a quinoa cereal?"

"Quinoa? What's that?"

"It's a wonderful grain from South America. It has lots of protein, it's gluten free, and it can be flaked." It sounded too good to be true, but I trusted her. She offered to create a few varieties.

The next week, the cereals were ready. She invited me to her house for breakfast. The presentation was beautiful: a linen tablecloth, napkins, fresh flowers in a crystal vase, bowls of cereal, milk, tea, and seasonal fruit. "Here you go," she said. "Dig in!"

Joanne had created four varieties containing quinoa and sorghum. "What's sorghum?" I asked.

"Oh, another gluten-free grain. It can't be flaked, but it can be milled. It adds a nice flavor."

We sampled the four varieties she'd made: Almond Blueberry Peach, Strawberry Mango, Orange Pecan, and Raspberry Coconut Pineapple. They all were delicious. "Wow, Joanne!" I exclaimed. "I think you've done it!"

The flavors were wonderful, and the texture was crunchy, but the new cereals didn't resemble granola at all. For one thing, quinoa flakes are tiny—quinoa is technically a seed. To produce the tender, thin flakes, the seeds are steamed and flattened. As with creation of the granola bars, Joanne had incorporated expensive ingredients. Dehydrated raspberries, for one. They were beautiful in the cereal and added wonderful flavor and a nice crunch. If SunDrops were nuggets of gold, dehydrated raspberries were nuggets of platinum. One variety had pecans, whose price had steadily gone up—it was one reason I'd discontinued the Pecan Granola. Lemon oil was a new ingredient and cost three times as much as orange oil. The quinoa flakes cost ten times as much as oat flakes. The dehydrated blueberries were expensive, as were the peaches, mangos, and pineapple. Joanne assured me, though, that because of the flavor intensity, only a small amount of the fruit and citrus oils was needed. "Okay," I sighed. What was my alternative? I couldn't disappoint my customers, and I didn't want to lose more of them.

Those dehydrated fruits were light as a feather. About a week after placing my order, a few enormous boxes—the size of refrigerator boxes—appeared at the bakery. "What can they be?" I wondered. "Perhaps I got someone else's delivery." I thought I wouldn't be able to lift them. But when I tried, I burst out laughing. They were my boxes all right—they just weighed hardly anything since so much moisture had been removed from the fruit.

A catchy name was necessary for this distinctive cereal. Off I went on a hike. By the end I had my answer: Quinoa Crunch. It was perfect, as it brought together the two most important features: it was crunchy and contained quinoa; the alliteration was an added perk. To contrast with the light-colored cereal and indicate a difference, I purchased brown window bags. Since it was "perfectly baked" and had "organic goodness in every bite," I did not create a new tagline. On the bags I added stickers reading: "GLUTEN FREE!"

That year at market, customers discovered the new cereals. And they liked them. I learned that people were willing to pay good money to have a gluten-free breakfast cereal. I also learned which varieties were popular and which weren't. Almond Blueberry Peach became our best seller, followed by Strawberry Mango, Orange Pecan, and Raspberry Coconut Pineapple. With space limited in the bakery, I narrowed the offerings. Orange Pecan was my personal favorite—delicate and full of flavor, with a subtle undertone of orange—but since the pecans and orange oil were expensive, I let it go, along with the Raspberry Coconut Pineapple. Raspberries were the most expensive fruit, and the pineapple clumped up after sitting around awhile.

Although the two remaining varieties sold well at market and on the website, I hesitated to present them to stores. After retail markup, the price would be 40 percent higher than my granola. They would likely be the first quinoa cereals on supermarket shelves, but still. At the end of the season, customers asked about availability in the stores. I decided what the heck—the grocery buyers could decide if the cost was too high.

When I next delivered to Whole Foods, I brought samples of the Almond Blueberry Peach and Strawberry Mango. Spice took one look at them and said, "Well, what do you have to lose, Fiona? The grocery guys might approve them, seeing as we don't have similar gluten-free cereals. More and more customers are asking for gluten-free products, so I think you've got a shot." Sure enough, Whole Foods approved the new cereals. They didn't fly off the shelves, but they sold well enough to keep from being discontinued.

I was tempted to market the Quinoa Crunch as a baby cereal. Soaked in warm water, it became a tasty porridge—soft and mushy just as babies need. The Strawberry Mango, since it didn't contain nuts, was allergy friendly. My idea was to package it into little pouch bags, similar to the pouch bags used for instant oatmeal. It would have been an expensive baby cereal. The Quinoa Crunch made a great breakfast to take camping. The cereal was light-weight, and with the addition of hot water, campers could enjoy a tasty, warm bowl of cereal packed with protein and other nutrients.

I didn't love the gluten-free offering I added to my line, but it was the best I could do at the time. Though they complained about the price, some customers got hooked. I explained about the expensive ingredients, and they understood. My customers were loyal; they kept me going.

*   *   *

One day at market, a French chef stopped by. He worked at the St. Julien, a high-end hotel downtown. Attached to the hotel was an equally high-end restaurant. My granola was on the menu there for both breakfast and Sunday brunch, and the hotel also bought the granola bars for business meetings. They were easy to offer as a snack during the breakout sessions, and attendees loved them.

"Hi there, Fiona!" the chef said. "How's business?" I said it was growing and doing well. He told me how much the restaurant clientele loved my granola, and that he thought we could expand the offerings. At the time, they were serving Almond Cranberry and Orange Crunch with fresh fruit and either milk or yogurt.

"I like granola and all," he explained, "but in France, we tend to eat muesli for breakfast. Do you know what muesli is?"

I nodded. "Yes, I'm quite familiar with muesli. I used to eat it in Germany. My favorite had hazelnuts and currants."

"In that case, do you think you could create a couple of varieties for me? No other restaurant in town offers muesli, and I'd like to add a European flair to the menu." I told him I'd see what I could do.

The following week, I perused the cereal aisles. When I read the muesli ingredients, I was appalled. "*This isn't muesli!*" I exclaimed out loud. The cereal manufacturers had added ingredients such as crispy rice, toasted oats, and twigs of bran. Genuine muesli has one distinguishing feature: It's raw. Muesli should not contain any ingredients that have been baked, fried, or toasted, yet there was not one muesli on the shelf that was completely raw.

Another important element is the absence of sweeteners, other than dried fruit; the muesli on the shelves contained brown sugar. And the final factor: Muesli is meant to be eaten raw. It is normally soaked in milk or yogurt to soften the oats; Europeans often immerse it in apple or orange juice. The muesli boxes in the supermarkets suggested that it be cooked like oatmeal. "Blasphemy!" I thought. Cooked muesli defeats the purpose of eating raw cereal.

I set out to create a true muesli. Raw. Unprocessed. Unrefined. Unsweetened. And simple. It didn't take long. I created three varieties, combining four ingredients—oats, seeds, dried fruit, and nuts—in different ways. Fruity Almond had rolled oats, whole flax seeds, raisins, cranberries, and sliced almonds; Cherry Pecan consisted of rolled oats, whole flax seeds, sour cherries, currants, and pecans; Pepita Papaya contained rolled oats, whole flax seeds, pepitas, golden raisins, and papaya. Today, pepitas are wildly popular, but at the time, green pumpkin seeds were not a common ingredient in food products.

As with my other creations, I solicited Natalie's opinion. I felt good about the first two varieties but was tempted to add coconut to the Pepita Papaya. I asked Natalie if we could run a blind taste test, and she agreed. Because she loved coconut, I thought that would be the version she'd prefer. Blindfolded, she diligently tried each sample—one from a clear glass, the other from a purple cup—alternating a spoonful at a time.

"Which one did you like best?" I eagerly asked as I took off her blindfold. She grabbed a pen and started writing:

"The clear glass cup was not as sweet as the purple cup. The oats seemed to stand out more then the purple cup oats. There was more fruit in the clear glass cup and more seeds. I like clear glass."

Then she wrote: "The purple cup was sweeter and the taste didin't call out to me like the clear glass did. It had less goodness to it and I'm suprised with myself because I didin't like the one with coconut." Along the bottom, she added: "I LOVE U! (MOM!)"

"Thanks, honey!" I gave her a big hug. "Your opinions are always helpful to me." Despite that she was only eight, I totally trusted her assessment: The Pepita Papaya would contain no coconut.

The French chef called the day after I dropped off samples. "Wow, Fiona, you've done it! This reminds me of what I used to eat in France. Thank you so much!"

The St. Julien added Fruity Almond to its menu, and Whole Foods took all the varieties, both packaged and in bulk. I gave the cereal a new tagline: "I'm Perfectly Raw!" Natalie loved the muesli, which she called "horse food" because she knew horses ate raw oats. Some mornings, she'd announce she wanted horse food for breakfast.

One day, Natalie presented me with a drawing she had made at school, titled, "The Moose Who Ate Moosely!" With colored pencils, she had drawn an adorable picture of a brown moose with green antlers, black feet, yellow eyes, and a pink tongue. One dialogue bubble said, "Yum! Yum!" and the other said, "Mooo!" An arrow pointed to a trough filled with cereal labeled "moosely"—one of her creative touches since she knew how to spell muesli. Above the moose she had added two butterfly stickers, and to complete the drawing, she had glued fresh leaves around the border as a frame. At the bottom, she wrote, "from Nat To Mom."

The gift showed that Natalie's mind stayed with the business more than I had imagined. I gave her a big hug and told her how much I loved it. She answered with a wide grin, pleased with her latest creation. I hung "The Moose Who Ate Moosely!" on the living room wall for all to see.

～9～
ADVENTURES IN CO-PACKING

"What matters is not length of life but depth of life."
—Ralph Waldo Emerson
(Quote on boxes of Ginger Walnut Granola)

U nsolicited advice was ever-present. One of the most common suggestions was to find a co-packer, something I had never heard of. The idea was to let me focus on sales and marketing rather than production, since co-packers are manufacturers who produce other companies' products. Smaller companies provide their recipes to the co-packers, theoretically leading to cost savings and a higher profit margin. The small company also has access to the large manufacturer's extensive distribution channels. If done well, both companies benefit.

Co-packers also offer private labeling. That, I learned, was the use of my recipes to manufacture products that would be packaged and branded under a different name. Some companies prefer not to dilute their own market share by allowing their recipes to be duplicated in this way, but the sales technique can be quite profitable.

I liked the co-packing idea. Dispose of my production headaches? It sounded too good to be true. Headaches I had, and plenty of them. My business was growing steadily, and I was barely keeping up. If my goal was continued growth, Howard's bakery would become too small, and I would need to find a new bakery, or a co-packer. With manufacturing out of the equation, my load could be lightened considerably. Product development and marketing were what I enjoyed most, so the ability to focus on those aspects of the business was equally tempting.

One day, I was doing a delivery at Whole Foods when I noticed two men in three-piece suits perusing the cereal aisle; they appeared to be there for something other than a shopping trip. Never one to let a sales opportunity go by, I walked up and said, "If you're looking for the best granola in the world, here it is!" and pointed to my packages. They seemed a bit startled. "I'm Fiona, and this is my granola."

"Oh?" one of them replied. "Is this a new line? I've never seen it before." I offered a quick synopsis of my company. After looking at me in silence for a few seconds, the man took a breath. "Perhaps this is serendipity," he said. "Your granola looks delicious, and much more appealing than the others." I learned that he managed two co-packing facilities in Los Angeles. "I'll buy a bag and see what I think," he said. "I'm always on the lookout for new cereals, and normally I'm disappointed with the granola offerings. I've always said that someone should make a really good granola." He grabbed a bag of Almond, I gave him my card, and we went our separate ways.

The next morning, at 7:30, my phone rang. "Fiona, this is Bill! I met you yesterday in Whole Foods. I'm the one who manages the baking facilities in California. This is the best granola I have ever eaten, and I've tried dozens of them." He asked about my sales, distribution, suppliers, and operations.

"Why don't you come out to California?" he asked. "I'd like you to see the facility, and we can bake a batch of your granola onsite. Your company has huge potential, and we could be your manufacturer." Bill's company co-packed for national brands such as Nabisco and Keebler. If he did right by them, certainly he could do right by me.

A few weeks later, I flew to California. Bill's company would bake Almond—what he called a "traditional" granola—and Orange Crunch. The company's facilities were enormous, each the size of a city block. Max, the master baker, was a food scientist who had been with the company a long time; he often helped small manufacturers with their product development.

During our tour of the facilities, I didn't notice many ovens. Bill said it was because most of the cereals were dehydrated. I told him I would insist on baking, emphasizing how important slow-roasting was to achieve the quality I wanted. He didn't seem too concerned. "We can certainly start off that way," he said. "But eventually, we'll have to move to the dehydrators. It's simply too time-consuming to bake and stir the granola once you get to a certain volume. It won't be cost effective." That was a huge concern, but I didn't say anything. The granola hadn't been made yet, so why get ahead of myself?

That afternoon, Max baked Almond and Orange Crunch granola. The next morning, when I tasted them, I almost choked. They were horrible! They didn't even resemble my granola. "Max," I asked, "did you use the ingredients I brought?"

"Yes," he replied.

"And did you follow my recipes?"

"Yes," he said. Then, after an uncomfortable pause, he cleared his throat. "Weell . . . I did substitute orange flavoring for the orange oil. That orange oil will be too expensive. The flavoring will do just fine, and no one will be able to tell the difference!"

I couldn't believe it. "That simply won't work!" I said. "I don't believe in flavorings. The reason the Orange Crunch is so good is because it's made with pure orange oil, not orange flavoring."

Bill and Max exchanged glances, and I didn't hide my frustration. "Any other changes I should be aware of?" I asked.

"Well," said Max, "I did alter the Almond recipe, just a little. I thought it was a bit flat, so I added some butter flavoring."

Butter flavoring! What was he thinking? "Max," I said as patiently as possible, "I don't want any artificial flavorings in my granola. I won't allow any recipe variations or ingredient substitutions." I asked if we could run another batch of each variety, this time following my recipes exactly. After some hesitation, they agreed.

When we got to the facility the next day, Chocolate Mint Clif Bars were being produced. The enormous mixers looked like cement trucks. In one of them, a worker reached inside with a superhero-sized spatula to scrape down the sides and empty the batter. From there, the dough went through an extruder, which formed the individual bars. They were transferred onto a belt, which passed through a tunnel oven where they baked. At the other end, they were cooled, packaged, and cased up. I had never seen such an operation and was mesmerized. Upon seeing my expression, Bill smiled and handed me a few bars, fresh from the production line. "Pretty cool, huh?" he asked. "Just think, that could be you some day."

Then we went upstairs to try the granola. It was awful. *Really* awful. Although Max insisted he'd followed my recipes exactly, the granola didn't resemble anything I had ever created. Producing granola this way would be cost-effective. I could reduce my prices and get into wider distribution. Fiona's could go nationwide, and I'd be a household name. But, at what price? I couldn't, with a clear conscience, offer a product that was not up to my standards, no matter the earning potential. I was proud of my food creations and accomplishments. I wasn't going to let my hard work be boiled down to a mediocre product that had my name on it. And I thought about my existing customers. I didn't plan to disappoint them by producing what would certainly be an inferior product. I had a reputation to uphold, and customers to keep happy. I took pride in both of those responsibilities.

I was grateful to have seen a co-packing operation. For many foods, the integrity and quality is not compromised, and co-packing is a good fit. For my products, it wasn't. When I returned to Boulder, I contacted Bill and thanked him for the opportunity. When I told him I would continue to manufacture my line, he understood—and was probably relieved. Producing the cereal to my specifications would have caused them problems. I would never agree to dehydrate the granola, use artificial ingredients, or speed up the curing process. No, it was best to continue on my own, using slow but proven manufacturing methods, and ingredients of my choosing.

*   *   *

One day, in need of a new baker, I stopped in at the Cooking School of the Rockies, which was next to Howard's bakery. I chatted a bit with Karen, the publicity director, whom I'd known as a member of the chamber of commerce. "By the way," she said, "we're putting on a gourmet French dinner next Friday night and have a spot open. Would you like to join us?" The event would be the students' final project, a lavish, multi-course dinner replete with white linen and fine wine.

"Thanks for the invite," I told her. "I'm sure it will be a wonderful dinner! But I have Natalie that night, and I don't like missing time with her."

"You mean that adorable daughter of yours?" she asked. She had met Natalie at the farmers market. "How old is she now?"

When I told her, she was silent for a moment. Then she asked, "Is she well behaved?"

"Oh, yes!" I replied. "She's very mature for her age."

She took a breath. "Oh, what the heck, if you think she'd enjoy it, then bring her along!" I couldn't believe it.

After learning about the invitation, Natalie broke into a smile and said she wanted to go. The evening of our dinner, she chose a colorful dress, white tights, shiny black shoes, and sparkly earrings. With her long blonde curls, bright blue eyes, and rosy lips, she looked like a china doll. At the table, we put two books and a pillow on the chair next to me so she could be the same height as everyone else. She chatted with the other guests and tried everything—from the homemade French cheeses and delicate *foie gras* to the tender *duck à l'orange* and roasted root vegetables. But her favorite course was dessert. The students had made long curly spoons out of sugar which they paired with fresh ice cream crafted from egg yolks, *crème fraîche*, and exotic flavorings. The dinner was truly memorable.

We decided a thank you card was in order. On my half, I thanked Karen for inviting us to such a gala event and told her how much we enjoyed the great food and company.

Natalie's half was much more interesting. She drew the dessert, putting elaborate detail on the homemade sugar spoon and scoops of ice cream. Above it she wrote, "What meal is this?!" And to the side, "All the meals were realy yummy!"

Instead of dots as part of the exclamation marks, she drew solid hearts. She embellished the card with squiggles and ended her note, "Love Natalie."

I was amused that Natalie called each course a "meal." For her little tummy, most of those courses probably did seem like a meal.

"This is just adorable!" Karen exclaimed upon seeing the card, which she promptly hung in the office. "Natalie is quite the artist." Although I never gained an employee from the culinary school, I was very happy to have popped in that day.

~10~
To Grow or Not to Grow?

"In wilderness is the preservation of the world."
—Henry David Thoreau
(Quote on boxes of Fruity Almond Muesli)

There are relationships in life that are difficult to process, and the stories hard to share. In the case of my granola business, the relationship had to do with someone who stepped into my life three and a half years after I started the company. The decisions made during the next two years came very close to bringing my company to a close.

I was at the farmers market one bright Saturday morning, early in the season. Though farmers were limited in their springtime offerings, warm weather had brought out a crowd. My booth was busy, and I was happily chatting with customers I hadn't seen all winter. I was alone that day, as Natalie was at her dad's.

I became aware of a young man quietly sampling the cereals, methodically tasting each one, intently with a great deal of focus. He seemed unaware I was watching him. After a few moments, I said, "Hello! Are you enjoying the cereals?"

He looked up, startled, and smiled. "Oh, yes! These are fantastic! In fact, I'm sure this is the best granola I've ever eaten. Did you create these? Are you Fiona?"

Thus began our first conversation, one that morphed into a business relationship that was to last almost two years.

His name was Rick, and he was new to Boulder. Though he worked as a CPA, what interested him was health and nutrition. He asked about the state of my business, number of employees, and plans for expansion. When he heard my answers, he asked, "Do you happen to need help? I'm looking to transition my career, and what you've got going intrigues me. I love the granola, and I think you've got great potential to grow this company. Since my background is in accounting, I could help with the books, budgeting, and other financial matters. And I'm a health fanatic, so I'd be a great advocate for this stuff. It could be really exciting!"

Rick's visit to my booth that morning was timely. I was exhausted from the demands of running the company. Other people had expressed similar interest over the years, offering marketing and sales assistance to help grow the business. Occasionally, I'd hired someone for this purpose. Isis was one, but she had only stayed a short while.

Former employees I'd hired—for tasks such as calling on accounts, delivering to stores, or performing demos—often resulted in more problems than assistance. Sometimes they got confused or didn't pay attention, leading to botched deliveries, shelves not stocked properly, and customer complaints about demos. Sometimes, employees lost invoices or did not rotate product. When my employees didn't follow store protocol or do as I had trained them, I ran the risk of losing accounts.

Store personnel asked that I do these tasks. I enjoyed them, and the personal relationships generated a lot of loyalty and goodwill, but it meant I was doing almost everything to run the business. Keeping up with so many duties was exhausting. Between that and taking care of Natalie, I had time to think only about the current day or the next. Long-term planning had not entered the picture, nor had I mapped out a direction in which to take my company.

I knew this kind of business management was not sustainable if I expected the company to grow. Some days, despite my earlier headaches with assistants, I was an open vessel ready and waiting for someone to jump in. That day at the market was one of them, and Rick's words were music to my ears. A young, bright, enthusiastic person with his kind of energy was just what I had hoped for.

Before he left my booth that morning, he added one more piece of information. "And you know, if the business is tight on cash, I'd be willing to work at no charge for a year. I'm in good shape financially, so it wouldn't be a burden. We could put an equity structure in place.

That way, you wouldn't have to disrupt your cash flow to pay me a salary. Anyway, think about it and let me know."

He took off, and I just stood there, dumbfounded. Could help be dropped onto my lap just like that, with absolutely no effort? I thought it too good to be true, but I chewed on the idea. Bringing on a business partner could have many advantages. Not only was Rick eager to jump in and help, but as an added perk, he spoke Spanish. Were any other qualifications necessary?

Our conversation caused me to think about the restraints of keeping my company small. Growing it would come with its own demands, but with a business partner, I would have help. Because I was so busy with day-to-day operations, I didn't think about expansion very often. I was happy to have ingredients and packaging on hand, capable bakers, well-made products, happy customers, stocked shelves, and paid invoices. As long as operations ran smoothly and I had quality time with Natalie, I was generally content to keep things as they were. The company was profitable, I paid myself considerably more than I'd earned at the chamber, the business's bank account grew steadily, and I had no debt. I worked around the clock, but I was the one who decided what to do and when to do it. I reminded myself that my flexible schedule was the reason I had started my company. My life was full, without worrying about fame and fortune. Nonetheless, I had always wondered what real growth would look like. Perhaps this was the opportunity to find out.

Within weeks of our conversation, Rick joined the company, informally, as a business associate. He assumed all responsibility for the company's finances, large and small—everything from payroll and bank deposits to bill payments and monthly reconciliation. They were duties I was relieved to pass off. When I occasionally asked him how the finances looked, he said that the balance sheet was healthy.

Howard did not care for Rick. There had been a few misunderstandings in the bakery, and they made Howard feel uneasy. Rick had a sharp sense of humor, which at times could be misread. I said that he meant well and apologized on his behalf; I also thanked Howard for sharing his concerns.

If I were to grow my company, I needed help. Earlier ideas to take my business to the next level hadn't met with success, nor had hiring employees to help with day-to-day activities. I had spent a good amount of time early on with consultants whose advice did not help grow my business. I worked with advisers who claimed they could take my product national, turn Fiona's into a household name, and thrust me to stardom—advise that came at a steep hourly price.

The advice I had received from consultants and potential investors did not resonate with my vision of the company. Their proposals were outside my comfort zone. They showed no indication they would listen to customer requests or allow room for flexibility and creativity. Fiona's Natural Foods would be run by someone other than me, with strict conditions. The idea was to choose growth strategies and tailor the line based on sales and efficiency.

I heard advice such as: "Don't expand your product line. You have too much going on. Just stick with granola and narrow your SKUs [meaning the variety of products]." Narrow my SKUs? I had developed each cereal variety with a purpose, keeping in mind my customers' food allergies and taste preferences. Two varieties were nut-free, two varieties were coconut–free, one was free of sesame seeds, and two did not have fruit. If I removed one of those types, I would lose customers.

Discontinuing everything except the granola was also not going to happen. I had created the other products based on customer requests. And they were a big hit. I wasn't willing to discontinue products that sold well and gave me additional shelf space in the stores. Those other products also helped to grow my brand. Discontinue my energy bars? They had a devoted following, and there were no others like them on the market. The same was true for the muesli and quinoa cereals. I was not going to disappoint my customers, especially when their ideas had led to the creation of viable products.

One adviser told me, "You give me 50 percent of your company, and based on my experience growing XYZ company, I will take Fiona's national. Since you don't have the expertise to grow a company, I'll be the CEO and you can be the creative director. The financial backers will also demand their share, but we'll be sure to make it fair for you."

I also heard other advice. "Be wary of investors—they'll take control of your company, which means you'll lose decision-making power." They could even vote me out altogether, I was warned. "Give away or sell enough of your company," one market customer warned, "and you—the original owner and creator—might be fired by the ones who then have control. It happens—and more often than you might imagine."

I had spent time and money with consultants, written a business plan, and allowed every aspect of my company to be analyzed. Based on growth and future potential, investors were extremely interested. Most were industry veterans, and they could have easily taken my company national. I had every opportunity to become financially wealthy. But their ideas did not complement mine. Since we couldn't see eye-to-eye, I turned them down.

The one investor I did consider was a respected natural food guru who had made millions in the industry. Shortly after I started the company, he said, "I'm intrigued with your granola. When I think of local entrepreneurs I'd like to invest in, you always come up. You're definitely on track." He asked to see my business plan and introduced me to industry consultants. He visited me regularly at market and bought two large bags of Almond granola each time. He said he ate it for breakfast every morning and shipped it far and wide to friends and other potential investors. One day at market, he said, "Come on over to the facility sometime to see our ovens. We can bake a ton of this in an hour." When he saw the surprised look on my face, he laughed. "If we come on as investors, it will be a fast ride, so you'll need to hold on tight." As tempting as the offer seemed, I didn't think I was up for that kind of ride.

I continued with Rick because I did not want to run the company alone. We didn't always agree on things, and our discussions were sometimes heated. He could be critical, and I could be stubborn. Still, he was a quick learner, took responsibilities off my shoulders, and shared the grunt work. Instead of focusing on the negative aspects of our business relationship, I kept to the belief that things would get better.

I also reminded myself of the many nice comments I had received. When I got discouraged, I dug out those notes, and their kind words helped to sustain my positive energy. One woman exclaimed, "You're gonna be the next Mrs. Fields! *Everyone* is saying this!" A woman who had been in my babysitting co-op said, "I can say I knew Fiona way back when." A vendor told me, "You're gonna be big someday, Fiona. It's a great story—small town girl makes good." One of my brokers said, "I think we're *all* going to do well with your line. I have complete confidence." The loyalty I felt toward my customers helped energize me as well.

As much as I enjoyed running the business, at times my brain was enveloped in fog due to continual sleep deprivation. There were also days I cried, mostly because of frustration and exhaustion. One consultant said it was "totally appropriate" and "part of the process." I shed plenty of tears in those years and was comforted knowing others did the same.

I often had a glass of wine or beer in the evenings; after a stressful day, the alcohol took the edge off and helped me to relax. At one point, Natalie became concerned that I was drinking a lot of beer. Truth told, I never drank more than two in one night. But to a child, that can seem like a lot. She'd watch with wide eyes as I opened the second bottle and say, "*Another* beer, mommy?! You sure are a beer fan these days!"

~11~

HIPPIE GRANOLA: BAGS TO BOXES

*"When we put our attention on something,
everything else will follow."*

—Anonymous

One day, at the opening of a new Whole Foods near Denver, I happened to see Scott, a regional grocery manager I'd met once before. "Hi, Fiona! How's it going?" I told him all was well.

"Yes," he replied, "we've been watching your sales. We're happy with the growth, and everyone at the home office agrees yours is the best granola out there." He smiled. "I eat it every chance I come to Colorado. I just can't get enough of that Orange Crunch."

I thanked him for his kind words, told him it was nice to see him, and said I needed to get back to my demo station.

"Yes, of course," he replied. "Before you go, I have a question. Would you be interested in getting into stores beyond Colorado?" A bit startled, I said yes but told him there was no distribution channel in place.

"Well," he said, "if you can put your granola into boxes instead of bags, I'll bring you into the entire region. And I'll get you set up with UNFI to take care of your distribution channel." I stood there in disbelief. *Bring me into the entire region?* And set me up with UNFI, the largest natural product distributor in the country? Wasn't this any small vendor's dream-come-true? I'd heard dozens of stories of vendors who had pulled out all the stops to accomplish this, often investing months if not years, and countless product samples, to make it happen. And here I stood, in an encounter I couldn't have planned, with the offer handed to me on a silver platter. Surprised and somewhat in shock, I just stood there, unable to speak. When he realized I didn't know what to say, he smiled and handed me his card. "Here," he said. "Let me know when you're ready." I thanked him, and we both went back to our duties.

My mind swirling, I did my best to stay focused during the rest of the demo. "Okay, I just need to make this happen," I thought. "The bags are driving me crazy anyway. They wrinkle easily and the windows tear if they're shuffled around too much. Plus, only a fool would decline an offer such as this."

Getting into distribution was *not* going to happen if I stayed in Howard's bakery, with its limited space for production and inventory. Boxes would also allow me to tell my story and educate consumers about the health benefits of my cereals.

I thought back to a conversation I'd had with a grocery manager at King Soopers, Colorado's largest grocery chain. "You don't want to put your granola in a bag—that's just suicide." Then he scanned the shelves with his index finger, from high to low. "See? If you want good shelf space, put the granola in boxes. Otherwise, it will end up on the bottom shelf, and I guarantee you, that's where you *don't* want it to be."

Up until then, I had been lucky. Since the granola was selling so well, grocery managers often placed it at eye-level. Still, I had a choice to make: Stay small, which meant I could stay at Howard's, or grow, which meant I would have to move.

Being part of a larger distribution chain appealed to me, partly because I was spending so much time with deliveries, taking a wider variety of goods to a growing number of accounts. I also shipped out website orders at least twice a week. I had put much of my life on the back burner for the good of the company; distribution could help build back some of that time.

I missed seeing old friends, like members of the babysitting co-op and the moms' hiking group I had joined when Natalie was four months old. For almost three years, we had gathered regularly for walks, hikes, picnics, and other activities. When I ran into a mother from one of these groups, usually at Whole Foods, it was fun to share family updates and reminisce. Most stayed at home with their kids, and I was the only one who'd gotten a divorce. I pined for their stay-at-home lives; why was I the only one splitting custody and working my butt off for a living? They made comments such as, "Wow, Fiona, you've made it really big with your granola company! Good for you! Your days must be so interesting. All I do is get together with other moms, cook and clean, and go to Target. I envy you!" It's true: The grass is always greener . . . .

* * *

Over the years, I participated in Expo West and Expo East, the largest natural product trade shows. For the first, I asked Natalie to create something artistic. After discussing ideas, she created six signs to highlight the cereal features. Markers in hand, she transformed the tops of six white energy bar caddies into colorful, whimsical pieces of art. "Organic!" was framed in a rainbow. "Salt Free!" showed a sun over the ocean with a bird flying overhead. "Dairy Free!" was punctuated by stars and happy faces. "Wheat Free!" was outlined with flowered vines. "Soy Free!" had a sun partially hidden by purple clouds, with lightning bolts and rain showers. "Gluten Free!" was lined with mountains that looked like the Andes, with fish and turtles swimming in the ocean.

My booth decor was simple: no glossy brochures, professional signage, or blown-up photos. On display were the cereal boxes, filled glass decanters, spoons, and paper cups; passersby could sample the cereals and take a sell sheet. Natalie's signs stood out and received many compliments.

My mother attended Expo West with me. The first year, we hung my logo that she had painted as a watercolor. The second year, we hung the logo in quilt form. We created a display and designed what we thought was an attractive booth. Not everyone agreed.

"If you stagger the heights of the boxes and decanters, it will make a more interesting presentation," one attendee commented.

"You need to add some interest to your booth," another said. "How about grouping the cereals together, so they are more easily distinguished?"

I took their comments in stride—I was doing the best I could with a limited budget, limited help, and limited time to prepare. Both years at Expo West, the local Boulder newspaper published articles about my participation, including a day-by-day "progress report" on booth attendance, distributor interest, and potential contracts with groceries. I appreciated the media coverage.

In addition to Natalie's artistic creations, she wrote numerous notes. When I first started the company, I was on the phone a lot. There was much to get organized and no way to control the timing of incoming calls. One afternoon, I was on the phone with Natalie sitting at the table across from me, quietly drawing. Out of the corner of my eye, I noticed a slip of paper sliding toward me. I picked it up and read, "I Love you mom! You are my favrit mom I ever had in my life! Wie do you hafe to make so meny phon calls? It is bering for me. Love Natalie"

My heart melted with the realization that even when she seemed happily occupied, she realized my attention was on someone else. Although only four, she didn't whine, cry, or become angry with me. Instead, she communicated her discontent by writing notes. I got off the phone as quickly as possible and promised I would do my best to not make or take business calls on her time. She gave me a big smile, and we had a long embrace.

Natalie usually turned to reading to keep herself occupied; she devoured almost any book she could get her hands on and read at a much higher level than her age standard. At the age of ten, she delved into *The Mists of Avalon*. But about halfway through, she lost interest. "There are too many characters," she said.

One reason she read so much is that the television in our house was used only as a "movie box." Together, we watched a wide variety of films. Alone, she watched Disney selections and shows such as *The Land Before Time*. One day, a visiting friend of hers ran to the television and exclaimed, "Let's watch TV!" Natalie's eyes opened wide, and she looked at me, frozen, not knowing how to respond. I walked to the television and softly removed her friend's hand from the button. "Actually," I told her, "we don't watch TV in this house. How would you like to choose an art project instead?" The girl looked confused, but after a few seconds said, "Okay! That sounds like fun!" Natalie let out a sigh of relief, and we exchanged smiles as they headed toward her bedroom.

*   *   *

A portion of my deliveries were already being made through a distributor. I had gotten my granola into the Sysco system, rather unexpectedly.

One day, the phone rang. "Is this Fiona?" The voice at the other end belonged to Truman, the operations manager for The Egg & I, a breakfast and lunch chain in Colorado, New Mexico, Texas, and Arizona. The restaurants had been buying their granola from an independent baker who had retired with little notice. Truman had found my granola after going to Whole Foods looking for a local replacement. "Wow, Fiona, this is really good granola!" he said. "In fact, I like it better than the other one. How large is your company? We're expanding, so I'd need to be sure you can keep up with production."

After I assured him that would be no problem, he said, "Okay. The other thing is, would you be willing to create a custom flavor just for us? We pride ourselves on made-from-scratch menu items. We say on the menu that the granola is "home-made," so we want to offer an artisan product that can't be found anywhere else."

We discussed ingredient combinations and settled on Cinnamon Almond Raisin. Finally, an account that wanted raisins!

"You got it," I told him. "I'll develop your granola this week." We set a time to meet, and I went back to my paperwork.

The following week, I drove to the chain's headquarters in Fort Collins. When he tried the granola, Truman broke into a wide grin. "This is fabulous!" he exclaimed. We signed paperwork on the spot.

A few days later, I heard the three-ring fax tone and saw the printer light up. It was my first Sysco order: 320 pounds of granola, packaged in ten-pound cases, to be delivered ten days later.

Later that week, I trained my employees to make the new variety. They baked the granola the night before delivery, dedicating the entire evening to that one variety. After loading my Subaru Outback with the thirty-two cases, off I drove to the Sysco warehouse in Denver.

Some employees looked at me suspiciously as I backed up on the little delivery ramp. I only chatted with them if they initiated conversation—I knew they were on the clock, and I thought it wise not to interfere with their schedules.

Inside, my eyes opened wide. I had never seen such a large warehouse, nor fork lifts that looked like golf carts zipping through the aisles, their drivers honking as they turned the corners. The warehouse employees eyed me also. When they spoke, they were brusque. "So, what ya got in those boxes?" Upon learning it was granola, they chuckled. "Granola, huh? I suppose it's healthy. No, not for me."

What filled the warehouse were pallets piled high with potato chips, corn chips, and every other imaginable snack—including things I had no idea people still ate, like Twinkies and Ding Dongs. My organic granola was surely one of the healthiest food at that warehouse. I smiled, knowing it had its very own slot amid all the conventional products laden with preservatives, colorings, and additives.

It was a man's world, a place of heavy lifting, cold temperatures, and gruff attitudes. Occasionally, one of the guys offered to fetch a pallet or help unload the cases, and we chatted while we worked. They'd make comments such as, "Hello, little lady. I see you brought us more of that hippie granola today." And, because they knew the cereal was made in Boulder, they'd add, "Are you sure you're not sneaking in a special ingredient?"

The receiver I chatted with the most called me "Maiden of the Earth." He'd see the dock door open and exclaim, "Ah, it's our Maiden of the Earth come to deliver more of that hippie granola!" The head receiver wasn't quite as pleasant. I couldn't check in with him until I'd loaded the granola onto two pallets and a receiver had counted them. I usually found him at his desk, shuffling through paper work. When he heard my friendly, "Hello there!" he'd slowly look up and say in his gruff manner, "Waz up, Hippie Chick?" His voice was deep and smoky and reminded me of John Wayne.

A few of the warehouse workers had noticed my custom license plate: GRANOLA. "Well, at least your license plate makes sense to me now!" they'd say. Or "That's pretty cool! Was it hard to get that plate? After all, this is Colorado. All those hippies would probably love to have your license plate."

I did love it. In Colorado, drivers can choose custom plates with up to seven characters. "That's perfect!" I thought. "I'll see if 'granola' is available." What were the chances? The hippie culture was alive and well in Colorado, and many people identified themselves as "granola heads." Surely someone up in Nederland or Ward or Eldorado Springs, little enclaves known for their hippie culture, had snagged that plate decades ago. When the Department of Motor Vehicles said it was available, I was stunned and ordered it that very afternoon. Over the years, I received many complementary, if not envious, comments. One man said, "You have the best license plate in Colorado." I was often asked, "Wow Fiona, how'd you pull that off?" I'd just smile and shrug, and say it was meant to be.

The granola sold well at The Egg & I, and the restaurant chain continued to open more locations. Within a few months, Truman called. "Fiona, can you double the quantity each time?" I gasped. "I'm not sure my Outback can hold that much. But I'll see what I can do." Amazingly, I managed to fit in sixty-four cases of granola. The car was packed to the gills and sagged from the weight, but it drove.

On warm days, by the time I got to the warehouse, my Subaru smelled like a brewery. At first, I couldn't figure out why. Then I realized it was the barley. When heated, it gives off that distinct aroma that permeates beer establishments. On Sysco delivery days, my car smelled like a microbrewery on wheels. Some days, the scent was so strong I had to roll down the windows.

Some years later, after Truman had left Sysco to open a coffee shop, the corporate office called. "We'd like to keep offering your granola, as it sells very well," the officer said. "But you'll have to up your liability insurance. You're at $1 million, but we now require $2 million from our vendors." I told him I'd take care of it. Although he expressed concern that I might not be able to keep up with their continued expansion, I never once missed a Sysco delivery. The Egg & I now has restaurants in over twenty states, and as far as I know, Fiona's Granola is served in all of them.

There was much to do before distribution through UNFI could begin. In the meantime, I enjoyed doing deliveries, as did Natalie. She especially enjoyed sorting through the bags—she'd tell me how many of each variety were there so I knew what to bring in the next time. During her counting, she offered commentary: "Mom, they're out of Almond Cranberry again! People must love that flavor." Or, "Guess what I found behind the row of Ginger Walnut? An Orange Crunch! How did that get there?" She was a good facer, meaning she tidied up the rows and put the varieties in their proper places.

Natalie had established a wonderful rapport with the grocery team members. When I did deliveries without her, I'd hear comments such as "Fiona, where's your little assistant?" or "Fiona, how's Natalie? I haven't seen her in a while."

*   *   *

When the time came to move from bags to boxes, I decided to find a graphic designer who specialized in food packaging. The flax cracker guys, whom I'd worked with at the catering facility and also knew from farmers market, had just transitioned their packaging from bags to boxes, and the look was spot-on.

I called their graphic designer, Al, and asked if he'd be like to design boxes for me. "Sure, Fiona, that sounds like a fun project," he replied. "I love your granola, and I think it will sell much better presented in boxes instead of those window bags. When would you like to come over?"

We met the following week. Al was relaxed and personable, and gained my respect immediately. I asked him to keep the logo large, put a window in the front, and keep the look clean and simple. I intended to max out the chance to communicate my message in what's called the package's "billboard space." Since my goal was to educate consumers, we would use those six box panels to tout the features and benefits of the product inside.

By that time, the granola was available in all the Whole Foods markets in Colorado. That had happened thanks to Louis, the store manager who had allowed me to give him a bag of my granola that night in his driveway. "Fiona, this granola is selling really well," he said when he saw me stocking product one day. "Are you in any of the other Colorado stores?" When he learned I wasn't, he made calls to the grocery buyers in the other stores, suggesting they bring it in.

Off I went, samples in hand. A few buyers balked at the prices since mine would be the most expensive in the store. I offered free fill to start, a case of each, which meant there was no risk. That worked, and each store brought in a few varieties, both bagged and bulk. My Local Vendor Profile was hung next to the cereals, together with tags that read, "I'm a local!"

Accounts in other parts of Colorado received a delivery once a week, through Jill. The granolas gained a decent following, and in high traffic stores, the cereals often sold out before the next week's delivery. As sales increased, most of the stores offered more shelf space. Jill also delivered to Vitamin Cottage and other health food stores, smoothie shops, and coffee shops.

One owner of a natural foods store in Colorado Springs called me after Jill had dropped off samples. "This is the most fabulous granola I have ever eaten or ever hope to eat! The flavor, the texture . . . there's no comparison. It's shocking it's so good!" She brought in every variety and they sold well.

Customer testimonials also continued. "I just love that Quinoa Crunch! I eat it like porridge, and I bread my chicken with it." Or "I love your granola with warm milk. It even stays crispy!" And "Thanks for creating the muesli. It reminds me of breakfast in Europe!"

Testimonials also came in via website orders. One woman wrote, "This is my favorite splurge food!" Hearing positive remarks from people outside of Colorado helped me to feel confident that the cereals could gain a wider following. A few even talked to grocery managers on my behalf and sent information to get the granola placed.

One day, a market vendor who stopped by my booth to barter said, "I've just walked the entire length of the market. And I've decided you're the happiest vendor on the entire street!" The enthusiasm and joy I felt in sharing my creations with the public, and in educating people about the health benefits, was hard to conceal.

Sometimes, though, the demos gave me a reverse educational opportunity. One day, a Canadian woman stopped by my table at Whole Foods. Without making eye contact, she picked up a bag of Almond Blueberry Peach Quinoa Crunch and read the ingredients. "So," she asked, "what's the natural flavoring?" I assured her it was an extract. She scoffed and said, "You know, in Canada, all ingredients must be disclosed. Consumers have a right to know what they put in their bodies. Don't you agree?" I said I did agree, but that I also wanted to protect my recipe. She set the bag down. "Well, she continued, "if I don't know what's in a product, I won't put it into my body." The woman smiled and walked away. I thought about our interaction and decided she was right. Before the first box production run, I changed "natural flavoring" to "pure almond extract." If someone wanted to steal the recipe, so be it. At least I could have a clear conscious enabling my customers to know exactly what they were putting into their bodies with each bite of cereal.

I was also looking at the same time to change the name of my Almond granola, the best-seller and the only cereal with just one "descriptor." I toyed with Almond Coconut and Coconut Almond but didn't want to risk turning away any potential new customers, since some people avoid coconut because of the saturated fat. With that in mind, I changed the name to Toasted Almond. Although all the granolas were toasted, the name had a nice ring to it.

By the time I switched to boxes, all my cereals were certified organic—at a time when very few others were. They also were wheat free, dairy free, soy free, and salt free. Agave was the only sweetener. For the boxes' front panel, we listed these attributes, along with the taglines specific to each cereal. We also included the Kosher symbol—to gain traction on the East Coast, I had undergone that certification process.

For the boxes' back panel, I shared a brief history and philosophy of my company, told a bit about our baking process, and—in a paragraph titled, "Did you know?"—described each variety's health benefits. To the side were illustrations Angela had drawn to distinguish two ingredients in each cereal. Al, my graphic designer, said a drawing of me on the box would help sales since customers could see there was "a real Fiona." I resisted; the idea seemed egotistical and self-indulgent to me. But others agreed with him, and alas, I conceded. If a personal image could help sell the cereals, why not? An artist friend in New Mexico did a wonderful job, based on a photo we took in Al's yard. Although I looked a bit like a twenty-year-old Barbie doll, Al thought the image was attractive, friendly, and helped to personalize the boxes.

I also added quotations to the packaging, on the top panel of each box variety, which I hoped would inspire my customers. Most were by well-known people, but a few came from anonymous sources. The side panels displayed information such as the nutrition panel, ingredients, and a health claim: "High in Fiber!" The bottom panel included the UPC code and recycle logo.

Al and I had fun choosing colors: Orange for Orange Crunch, brown for Cinnamon Almond, magenta for Almond Cranberry, red for Cherry Pecan, violet for Almond Blueberry Peach, pink for Strawberry Mango, rust for Cinnamon Raisin, gold for Ginger Walnut, teal for Fruity Almond and purple for Toasted Almond.

The final designs were beautiful. Simple, pleasing to the eye, and colorful. The white background would grab the eyes of customers as they perused the cereal aisle. I called them my Buddha boxes—set off by those gorgeous lotus flowers, they were short and stout, and happy to be their own incarnation.

Along with the box project, I was busy looking for new production space. There was no time to waste—Fiona's Natural Foods was growing, and quickly. There was a reason my company was ranked in Boulder County's "Top Ten Fastest Growing Businesses" and "Top 25 Women-Owned Businesses." Although the expanded product line increased revenue, it also added to our space constraints, which were already maxed out with ingredients and finished product. And the equipment we'd need for expansion also required space, both vertical and horizontal.

Loading my car for deliveries had become time-consuming, as Howard's bakery had no dock door. That meant quite a few trips in and out, especially after our Sysco orders went from thirty-two to sixty-four cases. The ingredients for our products were delivered by guys strong enough to throw fifty-pound bags over their shoulders. Each time I ordered a pallet of oats, in they came, two bags at a time, slung over Big Brian's shoulders. Brian was our main delivery guy; he stood 6-foot-4 and easily weighed twice what I did. He loved his job and was a jolly fellow. One day, he swiped me off the floor and flung me over his shoulder. "Very funny, Brian!" I yelled. "What do you think I am, a bag of oats?" He laughed and said, "Geez Fiona, you could be! You barely weigh more than *one* of those bags I just hauled in."

Occasionally, a would-be investor popped into the bakery to inquire about production, expansion, and to ask if I were looking for funding. Many were eager for a piece of the action and let me know they had cash to burn. I was tempted to see what growth might look like with a pile of money at my side, but after my co-packing experience, I was convinced that anyone with a vested interest in the company would keep the maximization of profits as their No. 1 goal. I was fiercely committed to the quality and integrity of my line, and had no plans to jeopardize my standards or agree to anything that did not resonate with my vision of the company. The investors who passed through the bakery were amazed at the quantity of product we manufactured in such a small space. I could see the wheels turning as they pondered what might be possible in a larger facility.

The advice they offered added to my apprehension. "Don't build out your own bakery," one of them suggested. "I realize you've outgrown this space, but you can put your ingredients in storage and bring them to the bakery as necessary. You can store your finished goods as well, and grab them as you need them for deliveries." Was he serious? That would have been a logistical nightmare, not to mention incredibly time-consuming. Others suggested co-packing, which I had thought about trying again.

Earlier in the year, I had contacted a large cereal manufacturer in Oregon. When I shared with the operations manager my first co-packing adventures, he seemed sympathetic. "Well, this is what we do for a living," he replied, "so I don't know why we couldn't do yours." I shipped the ingredients to them, along with baking instructions. To my dismay, their attempt to bake the granola turned out even worse than the first co-packer's. After that, I decided co-packing was not in the cards.

Some people suggested I build a bakery with other companies, sharing the cost and the ongoing expenses. The idea appealed to me, but I could already foresee production, cleaning, and scheduling headaches, not to mention possible legal problems. The best option, I decided, was to bankroll expansion on my own, and only use investors or bring in other companies as a last resort.

* * *

One morning, Rick and I were sitting outside a coffee shop in Boulder, meeting with Hunter, a commercial real estate agent who'd offered to help us find affordable space in or near Boulder. Hunter and I knew each other from the chamber. I liked his easy nature and professional demeanor. He was young and enthusiastic, and knew the market well.

In the middle of our conversation, a man approached the table and said, "Well, hello Fiona! I haven't seen you in a long time! How's business?" I looked up to see Don, the husband of my former boss at the chamber. The two of us went way back—we had spent our youths in the same little town in New Mexico, and we knew each other from the tennis courts. He eventually moved to Colorado, where he met my former boss. When we first saw each other at the chamber, some twenty years had gone by since our last encounter. In addition to the tennis connection, his parents had owned a small grocery where my grandmother shopped. The store carried European imports she could find only there.

Don had gone into finance, and he enjoyed a high position at the bank across the street from the coffee shop. I introduced him to the others and told him the nature of our meeting. "Oh!" he replied. "Congratulations on the expansion. That's very exciting! I suppose you'll be needing some money?"

"Oh, I'm sure we'll need plenty of that," I told him. "We were just discussing the high costs of building out a facility here."

"Well, when you're ready, give me a call. I'd be happy to see what I can do." He gave me his card and took off.

The three of us just looked at each other, stunned. If he only knew how hard we had tried to secure a business loan. The banks wouldn't even talk to us. I had set Rick on that task from the beginning. Since he was a CPA, I reasoned, he must understand how to fill out those forms and secure funding. Despite his efforts, though, bank after bank turned us down. Not enough time in business, not enough collateral, not enough money in our bank accounts, too much risk. Even with $50,000 in the business bank account, sales steadily on the rise, and no debt, even my current bank turned us down. I had convinced myself we would have to go the investor route to get more capital, appealing or not.

The search for new bakery space began. Hunter was all over it. He showed us possibilities in both Boulder and the surrounding towns. Because of cost, size, location, and other constraints, the available spaces didn't work. The only viable space we found shared a common wall with a marijuana-growing facility. That idea didn't bother me, but the smell did. It was intense. So were the security requirements. Because of the common wall, we were advised to use heavy locks and cameras. If someone broke into our unit to access the pot on the other side, we might be held liable. My venture would be risky enough. I didn't need to increase the risk by locating on the other side of a grow facility.

In the end, we leased space in Louisville. Because the towns surrounding Boulder don't possess the same panache, the cost of living and doing business there is considerably lower. The commute would be longer, but the rent savings would make up for it. I would also have an office as part of the deal.

I had worked from home since starting the company, using the loft in our condo as an office and play area for Natalie. I loved sharing the space with her. She had her little round table and chairs there, and a small desk. Her chest of stuffed animals and a pile of books were in one corner, along with her art supplies. The loft had a slanted roof, so as Natalie grew taller, we moved her desk to accommodate her new height. Our dog, Jouey, also shared the space—his old age and arthritis meant we had to carry him up the stairs to the loft. I would continue to use the home office, for sure. But the opportunity to more clearly define my personal life and my business life appealed to me. Perhaps I could occasionally leave my work at the new bakery. What a concept!

Hunter found space that seemed too good to be true. He had previously worked with the landlord, Steve, who was intrigued by the concept. He had constructed commercial sites all over Boulder County but had never built one for food manufacturing. He was a health nut and an athlete. I assured him we'd provide as much granola as he could eat. He was friendly, helpful, fair, and easy to work with.

Alas, after three wonderful years, my time at Howard's bakery came to an end. What was surely a relief for him was sadness for me. But the move was necessary for my company to grow. In our new space, though, I felt trepidation from the beginning. Not about the bakery, nor about Steve. Mostly I felt nervous about our bank loan.

True to his word, Don had come through for us; he had clout at the bank and wasn't afraid to use it. The loan was considered a risky one—my company was young and the bank believed sales were not high enough—but it filled in those gaps with what Don called "goodwill." This was based on the company's potential growth and my personal relationship with Don. Goodwill aside, though, I was required to list my condo as collateral. My parents worried: If we lost the condo, where would Natalie and I live? Would I lose parenting time? These thoughts also raced through my mind, but I kept them moving. Out of my head they went, because I couldn't bear to think that way. Everything would be fine. That became my mantra: *"Everything will be fine."* I had a business to grow, a bakery to build out, employees to manage, and products to develop. Most important, I had a daughter to raise. If I could stay focused, keep a positive outlook, not worry, and not lose sight of the wonderful opportunity that lay before me, *everything would be fine*.

The space was much bigger than needed, but it was the closest we could find to suit our needs and allow for expansion. Steve suggested we share the space. After opening the first loan statement, I was very much on board with the idea. But Rick rejected it immediately. "Just think of the production headaches, potential ingredient theft, cleaning issues, and equipment liabilities," he said. "No way, it's too much of a risk."

Being the only tenant was less complicated, but that luxury came at a high price. In addition to the $3,610 monthly loan payment, we had an even higher rent plus a multitude of other expenses, including a security system I didn't think we needed. We were one unit of six, and the entire building had motion detector lighting. But Rick insisted, and I acquiesced. I also agreed that we would remain the only renters.

The bakery under way, it was time to shop for equipment. A former consultant of mine knew a broker named Victor who had grown up in huge bakeries and supposedly knew equipment like no one's business. An introduction was made, and Victor scheduled a trip to Colorado. He was pleasant enough, wasn't a fast-talking salesman, and seemed to understand my budget constraints.

Victor pushed for a tunnel oven, but having seen them in California, I questioned his assessment. "Victor, we hand-stir our cereals during the baking process," I explained. "I bet those stir stations won't break up the granola enough to allow it to brown evenly. For the granola to dry out properly, air needs to circulate through the entire mass, not just penetrate the surface."

For each of my concerns, he had a solution. "Oh, you should see what tunnel ovens can do these days! There are many options. We can install as many stir stations as you'd like. With enough of them, the granola will break up and dry out."

When I asked what size oven he had in mind, he said there happened to be one in his warehouse that was the perfect length: fifty feet.

"*Fifty feet?*" I asked. "That's not long enough to allow time for the granola to brown nicely. I'm not sure it will even dry out before it gets to the end."

"Well," he replied, "that's why you set the belt speed on a verrry slow setting. You can set the speed so the granola takes an hour to pass through if you'd like."

I asked what happens when the granola gets to the other end. "Well, from there, it falls into a bin. Buckets attached to a conveyor belt gather it up, and the filled buckets pass under a fan so the granola can cool quickly." I did my best to visualize this. "The buckets then continue to a vertical hopper," he went on. "The granola empties into the hopper, then falls onto rotating scales that sit on top of the pack-aging equipment. The desired quantity drops down the chute and is sealed in the bags."

By this point, not only was my head spinning but I also didn't like what I was hearing. "Victor, that process simply won't work," I told him. "We let the granola cool overnight before packaging. Magic hap-pens when it cools slowly. If we pass it under fans to cool, the granola simply won't taste as good."

He looked at me with a long stare. "So is the idea to upscale your production or not? You simply can't grow a company without adjusting to a more efficient production process. Do you really want to slow the process down that much, just to let the granola cool on its own?"

I didn't answer. He took a breath. "Have you ever tried cooling it with fans?"

"No," I conceded. There was a moment of silence.

"Okay," I said, "assuming we go ahead with the fans, what happens after the granola is packaged into the bags?"

"From there," he said, "the bags are placed in a cartoner. The cartoner opens the boxes, pushes the bags inside, seals the boxes, and stamps the expiration date on the outside." That was easy enough to picture.

"Then," he continued, "for added efficiency, we'll get you a caser."

"What's a caser?"

"It's a machine that opens the case packs, places the boxes inside, and seals them up. They're real time-savers, and not expensive."

Enough for that day's Equipment 101 class. I'd absorbed all I could. All I saw were dollar signs—and the satisfied look on Victor's face for the education he'd just imparted.

Feeling limited by time constraints, I agreed to Victor's plan. Whole Foods wouldn't wait for the boxes indefinitely.

He had the perfect tunnel oven, he said, for a "really good" price. How much? I asked.

Twenty thousand dollars.

"Twenty thousand dollars for a used oven!" I thought. "He must be crazy."

Perhaps so, but he was also a good salesman. He assured me the equipment was in great shape, and agreed to cover shipping.

He created a detailed equipment list with two columns: "C" for Critical and "N" for Nice to Have. Various items in his "C" list didn't seem so in my mind, and equipment listed under "N" were necessary to produce granola. Later, I wondered if his "C" list were those items he most desperately wanted out of his inventory.

Victor confessed that the tunnel oven had been in his warehouse "for a while" and would need "a few minor repairs." He sold us a double rack oven to use in the meantime. It accommodated forty-four large sheet trays, which he also had on hand, but their sides were too low for us to mix the ingredients in the trays. However, Victor had the perfect piece of equipment for that: a ribbon blender, which would gently mix the ingredients as they tossed about in its large cavity. "Just think of the labor you'll save!" he exclaimed. "No more mixing those ingredients by hand!"

We purchased the bucket elevator, vertical form-and-fill, parts for the tunnel oven, and two large hoses to clean the ribbon blender. The builders installed a floor sink to allow the water to drain into the ground; they installed another underneath our three-part sink, which Victor also sold us. Holes had to be drilled into the cement to install the floor sinks—the procedure was loud, dirty, and expensive.

What I didn't buy from Victor came from bakery auctions and on-line; equipment was plentiful, as the "low-carb" craze had set in, causing bakeries to close right and left. We purchased a Hobart mixer, pallet racks, air compressor, walk-in cooler, shelving, fork lift, pallet jack, wooden production table, stainless steel counters, oven racks, walk-in cooler, stainless steel drums, air storage tank, and more.

We also purchased a state-of-the-art dock screen door for nineteen hundred dollars, which Rick found. It was exorbitant, much more extravagant than we needed. I found a different one, not so fancy, that cost half as much. But we ended up buying his door. It simply wasn't an issue worth battling over.

We also bought an elaborate phone system for three thousand dollars. Including the production area, which Rick wanted, meant a considerable amount of wiring and installation fees. He also suggested an intercom system so we didn't have to leave our offices to talk with employees in the production area. It seemed excessive, but I acquiesced.

Smaller ticket items included utensils, cleaning products, bathroom supplies, oven mitts, floor mats, brooms, mops, buckets, trash and re-cycle containers, and rodent stations. I preferred the rodents be caught in a humane way and released, but was not an option. Happily, we never found any rodents in those flat metal traps. Other expenses in-cluded tenant occupancy fees such as landscaping, snow removal, ex-terior pest control, and building maintenance. We bought office furniture, brand-new, that Rick found at Office Depot, and assembled it ourselves, which saved a bit of money.

I'm a color fanatic. Every place I've lived, big and small, has been filled with color, usually a different one for each room. Part of this has to do with my love for ethnic-type decor, which is usually rich in color and texture. Part of it is my belief in feng shui, which holds that dif-ferent colors impart different energies. Colors also lend ambience. I would be spending a lot of time at the bakery, and wanted to feel com-fortable in my surroundings. I also wanted to offer a cheery, colorful work environment for my employees. There would be no dull gray walls. I was after light and bright.

I researched color psychology and learned that employees are most productive when surrounded by yellow. It's not a color I'm a fan of, but I love gold. Steve and I chose a gold that had a bit of or-ange in it, which added depth and an invigorating feel. Not only was our five thousand square feet of production space surrounded by a deep orangey-gold, but sunlight poured through the windows that lined the walls. Walking into that production area was like walk-ing into sunshine. The space was bright, colorful, and energizing. I was convinced it was the most beautiful production area in all of Boulder County.

We also painted our offices, the hallway, and the break room with different colors. Rick thought the paint was extravagant. Perhaps it was, but compared with our other purchases, the cost of paint and painters seemed inconsequential. I would feel happier and more at home surrounded by color.

When the build-out was complete, we had a beautiful new bakery: sunny offices, bright production space, and a big break room complete with full-size refrigerator, microwave, double sink, table and chairs. We even had his and hers restrooms. Theoretically, we had a tidy operation, ready to go and poised for growth.

~12~
FACTORY FIASCOS

"What we think, we become."

—The Buddha

Week after week, equipment arrived from Victor's Warehouse of Used Goods. I felt like a little kid at my own birthday party, eagerly anticipating what might be in those crates, and convinced it would be bright and sparkly and just what I wanted. Instead, as each box was opened, my heart sank. What emerged—crate after crate—was beat-up equipment, battered parts, and scuffed-up utensils. After the equipment was installed and for the most part operational, Victor took his leave. He generously left behind one of his prized tool kits, "just in case you'll need to do any repairs along the way."

The few new items we bought contrasted with their battered counterparts from Victor, creating an eclectic display of goods. The juxtaposition of dull and tattered equipment against the backdrop of freshly painted, golden-orange walls, was not easy to behold. However, to my relief, most of the used equipment was functional. The rack oven worked like a dream and let us bake four times as much granola as we'd baked with Howard's oven. The ribbon blender worked great, as did the Hobart mixer, forklift, and pallet jack.

Life in the bakery, for the most part, was functional. We could efficiently produce the granola, Quinoa Crunch, muesli, and energy bars. The ribbon blender mixed the muesli in a heartbeat. Then I checked whether the prototype cereal boxes I'd ordered worked with the cartoner. Compatibility, *not happening*. The boxes didn't fall squarely through the chute, which meant they didn't open properly. When they exited, the corners were bent and uneven. The glue pot didn't hold the proper temperature, which prevented the boxes from sealing correctly. Victor returned to Colorado to work on the cartoner. He banged and hammered and fiddled around for days but was never able to make it functional. Back it went.

The next dud: the caser. The metal arms were so badly bent they deformed the cases instead of grabbing and opening them. We knew the bent arms would also mangle the retail boxes in the attempt to grab them and insert them into the case pack. Despite Victor's best efforts to straighten those arms—and the loss of hundreds of boxes in test runs—we gave up. That piece of equipment had been a luxury to begin with, so I wasn't sad to see it go. Manually packaging the retail boxes into cases was not a big deal, and for the bit of time the caser may have saved, I preferred to save the money.

The bucket elevator looked like a museum relic. The rails were so badly bent that the buckets could barely make it from the oven to the vertical form-and-fill machine. They wobbled along their track but looked as if they might tip over at any moment. And their destination? That was another fiasco. The form-and-fill machine was not functional. The scale at the top didn't work, the chute was too narrow to allow clumps of granola to pass through, and the film mangled, preventing it from forming into bags. Back it went. We hoped the compressor and storage tank were in good shape but couldn't be sure because the pieces of equipment that depended on their use were not in working order.

The walk-in cooler was functional but problematic; between assembly, electrical hookups and repairs, it had already cost an extra $1,000, and the vent continued to leak. Eventually we put a bucket underneath and arranged ingredients to avoid contact with the water drops. We decided to live with a drippy vent and slight variations in temperature and humidity.

Victor had convinced us to buy a nut grinder, assuring me of huge savings if we ground our own peanuts and almonds for the energy bars. "The grinder works great. You simply pour the nuts in there, and *voila!* Out comes creamy, consistent nut butter for about half the price of premade butters." I had already tried that method based on the same advice from Joanne. However, Victor's was industrial strength and might just do the trick. But, in addition to taking up a huge amount of space, it turned out to be useless. Oil from the nuts leaked out, it was hard to clean, and the motor was shot. So long, nut grinder.

The tunnel oven was a thorn in my side from the minute I set eyes on it. It arrived in five huge crates, and Victor worked with an oven expert for months to assemble it. There were problems with the heating mechanism, the edges weren't high enough to keep cereal from spilling out, the band buckled, and every so often the conveyor belt stopped, trapping the cereal inside. The final blow: There were no stir stations. Victor said they would be easy to install, but his claims no longer instilled confidence. My patience, already worn thin, continued to unravel. Some days, I resembled one of the frayed electrical wires visible throughout the bakery.

After six months, Victor gave up on the oven. Between airfare, car rental, hotel stays, meal expenses, and the time he was spending in Louisville, it was costing him a lot. At one point, he hired Jacques, a French-Canadian, to take over. Jacques was a breath of fresh air—calm, personable, and knowledgeable. His presence soothed my nerves and gave me hope the oven would soon be functional. But after weeks of trying, not even Jacques could get it to work properly.

My patience had expired, and with it, my last drop of goodwill. I told Victor to get that oven out, *pronto*. He balked, knowing what a huge job it would be. After all his effort and expenses, he wanted some kind of return on his investment. He hemmed and hawed and offered excuses as to why he couldn't remove it. His dithering wasn't the only thing that brought my tolerance to an end. As if all the equipment fiascos weren't enough, he couldn't get my name right. He insisted on calling me "Theona." As often as I corrected him, his memory dislodged the information. Despite my company name of Fiona's Natural Foods, his equipment proposals were addressed to "Theona's Fine Foods."

Because we paid only for the equipment we kept, Victor absorbed the cost of shipping the faulty pieces back to his warehouse. He wasn't pleased, but I wasn't a happy camper either. We'd bought parts and covered other costs that should have been his. I kept a running tab in the hope the expenses would be reimbursed someday. My No. 1 goal was to finish the new bakery and have it operational as quickly as possible.

Steve was a saving grace. He visited the bakery to check on our progress and see if we needed anything. When he saw something questionable, such as the location of hanging electrical outlets, he alerted me. The pieces of equipment didn't always stay in the spots originally intended for them, which meant cables were scattered randomly about. Steve kept a calm demeanor, which helped soothe my frazzled nerves. I trusted him and knew he was keeping my best interests in mind.

Another saving grace was that none of my employees quit during that time. My aggravation, together with the delays and palpable tension that permeated our space, had to affect them. I worried that the shenanigans would cause them to lose respect for me and my company. Luckily, they kept doing their jobs despite the understandable distractions of the constant activity.

Victor's Equipment Carnival had one last act: Plead with me to keep the oven, because surely I could find someone to make it functional. I was furious. He had played Music Man one too many times, and I had reached my limit. That oven had come with a huge price tag, and after such a steep negative return on our investment, I did not intend to keep it. Financially, it cost electricity usage, installation fees, labor, and machinery parts. Operationally, it cost months of lost time. Emotionally, it cost frustration, anger, and exasperation. I told him the oven would not remain in our bakery. After a few heated discussions, we reached resolution. The oven would stay, but we could try to sell it. If we found a buyer, we could keep the proceeds. If we couldn't, we would tear it down, at our expense, and haul it piece by piece to the large trash receptacles behind the bakery. Although Victor had also invested a considerable amount, the last thing he wanted to do was ship it back to his warehouse. Our keeping it saved him dismantling fees, shipping fees, warehouse fees, and the headaches that would surely come with disassembly.

Because of the equipment duds, it wasn't hard for Rick to convince me to replace them with brand new equipment. Lee, the equipment broker he found, was friendly enough. He made suggestions, and even though his pay was mostly commission, he didn't try to convince us to purchase more than necessary.

First order of business was a vertical form-and-fill machine. Rick pushed for an expensive model which came with every bell and whistle. Even Lee thought it was more than we needed, but Rick convinced me that our sales would grow quickly enough to warrant the added expense. Lee sold us a cartoner and incline conveyor, and the rest of the equipment we found online.

Even with the bank loan and steady sales revenues, funds were tight. Build-out costs continued to escalate, mostly because of the adjustments Steve's crew had to make to support the new equipment. I was determined to keep up with our loan payments, which meant sales had to stay strong.

One day, the phone rang. It was Shelly, Don's assistant at the bank. "Hi, Fiona! How's biz? Is everything going well at the new facility?"

I couldn't bear to tell her the truth. "Oh, yes!" I exclaimed. "Things are going great!"

She seemed relieved. "I'm so glad to hear that! I called to let you know that you qualify for a little more money, seeing as your collateral is so strong. Do you have what you need, or would you like to borrow a little more?"

"Borrow *more*?" I thought. *Heavens, no.* I was already uneasy with the size of our loan, not to mention our ever-lengthening expense sheet. I thanked Shelly for the offer but politely turned it down.

The following week, Steve presented me with an invoice—for a project that hadn't been necessary originally but was needed because of the added equipment requirements. The amount: $10,000. My heart sank. "Not another build-out expense!" I thought. "Will they ever stop?"

The next day, I made the grave mistake of mentioning to Rick that we could borrow more money from the bank. "Are you *serious*?" he asked as his face lit up. "Of course we need to take whatever they'll offer. What great news!"

"*Great news?*" I thought. My collateral was already on the line; I didn't want to dig out of even more debt. I had taken the original financial risk because I was so far into the process, I just couldn't give up. How could I turn down Whole Foods' offer to bring my granola into the entire region? I had loyal customers and loyal accounts, and my company had the potential to go national. But, we needed a bakery that could support that kind of growth. I had come this far. How could I not see it through?

We took out the second loan—ignoring what every cell in my body said to do. I was increasingly uneasy about the entire endeavor; I started to experience anxiety, depression, and occasional panic attacks. I was sleep deprived, developed food allergies, and lost weight, all adding to my stress. I needed to be confident and resilient, but most days, those feelings eluded me.

~13~
ROO THE SUBARU

"Focus on the beauty, and expand upon it."
—Anonymous
(Quote on boxes of Almond Blueberry Peach Quinoa Crunch)

The months passed and spring was upon us, which meant the next season of farmers market was right behind. With the move, build-out challenges, equipment hassles, new employees, graphic design deadlines, packaging issues, and added commute time, my days were hectic and over before I knew it.

Natalie was a soccer player, so the days she was with me, I left the bakery early to get her to practice. Once there, I stayed. I loved those days. They got me out of the bakery and into the fresh air and sunshine, and I was surrounded by happy children running around the soccer field. I took that time to decompress, relax, and enjoy time with my daughter. Seeing the camaraderie, team spirit, and downright fun these kids had was a real treat and a welcome escape from my stressful days. Natalie loved it when I stayed at practice, and I think the other kids did too. Only occasionally did other parents stay after dropping off their children, so my presence was a bit of a novelty.

One day, I got to school later than I had planned. I discovered Natalie sitting at one of the long cafeteria tables, drawing. She looked abandoned and forlorn. Except for the counselors, she was alone in the room. I told her I was sorry I'd gotten to school so late. "Mom," she said, "I don't want to be the last kid to get picked up anymore. It's no fun here without any friends to play with." Her sincerity shot a dart right through me. Feeling as if I had screwed up my priorities once again, my eyes welled up with tears. I took her hands into mine. "I'm so sorry, honey," I replied. "I'll make sure to get here earlier from now on." She perked up and asked me to promise that I would, which I did. She let loose a big smile.

I felt grateful she liked the after-school program. The kids there learned about caring, sharing, and treating their peers with respect, in ways they didn't learn in the classroom. They were encouraged to unleash their creativity, participating in art projects, theatrical performances, games, sharing circles, and outside playtime. New friendships were established, and the older kids took the younger ones under their wing and helped them with their homework. It was a comfortable, fun, and happy place for Natalie to spend time after school. There was a quiet corner just for reading, which was where I often found her.

Occasionally over the years, Natalie's teachers asked if I would participate in a baking class with her schoolmates. I obliged, quite happily. Our first class was at the Montessori preschool. We baked a huge batch of granola at a long table where the kids created their art projects. In elementary school, we made granola bars with Natalie's Girl Scout troupe and for "Healthy Foods Week." When she was in middle school, I spoke to one of her classes about entrepreneurship and the process of creating my company. I always enjoyed participating in school activities with Natalie and her classmates.

One evening after dinner, we were sitting at the table together. Natalie was doing homework and I was filling out paperwork for the farmers market. "I can't wait for market to start up again," she said. "Will we be in the same spot as last year?" I told her I wasn't sure, and asked if she liked that spot.

"I do," she said. "It's close to Art Stop, and I like being next to Chad." Chad ran the mushroom booth. "I also like that we're close to where I get picked up for my soccer games." Natalie's games were on Saturday mornings, which meant I missed most of them. Our booth space was almost at the end of the street that passed through the market. Whoever was picking her up would drive to the corner, where Natalie and I were waiting. I always gave her energy bars or a bag of granola to offer to the driver, who was normally another mom with her own kids in tow. Before I knew it, she was back—tired, happy, and hungry, telling me about the "yucky" snacks at the game that day, and the "unhealthy drinks." I let Natalie eat whatever she wanted when she was with others; I didn't want her to feel deprived if there were donuts or sugar-laden cookies or pouches of artificial juice going around. But for the most part, she chose to stay away from all that. Her favorite soccer treats were bagels and fresh fruit. No matter the food offerings, once back at market, she was eager to head up the street for her dumpling fix.

Shortly after Natalie's eighth birthday, we created a product together based on her idea. We named the concoctions Natalie's Chocolate Clusters. We stirred nuts and dried fruit into melted chocolate chips, resulting in varieties such as Blueberry Pecan, Cranberry Almond, and Raisin Peanut. They were delicious and simple, and we were sure they'd be a big hit with our market customers.

One Friday evening, we made a bunch of chocolate clusters, created cute labels, and packaged them to sell the next day at market. Customers expressed delight at Natalie's creations, and a few of them made purchases. However, as the day wore on, the clusters became a challenge. The day was much warmer than forecast, melting the chocolate in its packages—not exactly an attractive presentation. When we chilled them in our cooler, the chocolate turned gray and waxy, which was equally unattractive. Fluctuating weather patterns would make it difficult to keep the chocolate at a good temperature, so we let them go. In the weeks that followed, with disappointed hearts but happy taste buds, the two of us polished off every last cluster.

One Saturday, Natalie returned from Art Stop, beaming. "Mom, I had so much fun this morning!" she exclaimed. "Look, I made you a book!" It was entitled "My Farmer's Market Diary." She had taken two yellow pieces of construction paper, cut them to a suitable size, punched five holes along one edge, and inserted five pieces of plain white paper, which she punched holes in to align with the cover. She threaded orange yarn through the holes and tied the ends into knots.

"I want you to write this book tonight after I go to bed," she instructed me. "You can tell about all the things that happened today at market!" I gave her a big hug and kiss and told her how much I loved my book. I promised I would write it that night.

I dutifully filled in all the pages. I listed friends who had stopped by, jotted down what goods we bartered, and recorded what we had for lunch and how much product we sold. I described the weather, noted that we ran out of Magical Mocha bars, and mentioned our excitement to try the season's first peaches. The book ended with, "All in all, it was a great day at market!" The next morning, Natalie's first words were, "Did you write the book?"

"Yes," I replied with a smile. "And I so enjoyed it." She seemed pleased with the finished product; I set it next to a photo of the two of us on our bookcase, for all to see.

Although Natalie was a happy child, her life was not easy. As much as I tried to shelter her from my daily stress and worries, they were not easy to mask, and her other household came with its own share of tension. Added to that, she went back and forth between homes every few days—not easy for anyone, much less a child in elementary school. I wished more than anything that she didn't have so much to contend with. But there was nothing to be done about it, so we all dealt with things the best we could. For Natalie, her ubiquitous pile of books kept her mind happily occupied.

Her fantasy world was another form of escape. She started reading *Harry Potter* in the first grade, and she devoured each new book as it came out. Like a lot of kids, she read them multiple times. Her "dragonology" collection included stuffed dragons, colorful wands, vessels to hold magic formulas, incantation booklets, charms and amulets, dragon games, and richly illustrated books that revealed dragon history, legend, and lore. Natalie's fantasy world was ever-evolving. In her backpack, she carried little notebooks dedicated to her magic. She and her friend Leah created characters with various powers, and they made up spells, verses, and charms. During elementary school, they got comfortable in a corner of the cafeteria in the after-school program and played made-up games for hours. Natalie didn't share much of this world with me—it was an area of her life I wasn't privy to, and I respected that. Every so often she mentioned a new character they had invented, or a new spell they had put on someone.

I made it a habit to check the "Mood-o-Meter" Natalie had hung outside her bedroom door. She'd made this piece of art in kindergarten; it had a dial that could be pointed to various moods, which ranged from sad to glad to mad. If I didn't hear activity for a while, I tiptoed to her bedroom to check the meter—she was good about updating it. The arrow almost always pointed to "happy," but occasionally she rotated it to "angry" or "quiet." Pretty much 100 percent of the time when I checked on her, she was lying on her bed, happily reading. After chatting a few minutes, she was eager to return to what she'd been doing.

One effective use of her creative talents involved Chad, our booth neighbor at farmers market. He was a fellow soccer player and took an interest in Natalie's games. They got along well, and he often let her hang out at his booth. He even paid her $5 an hour to weigh mushrooms, which added to her enthusiasm to help. One season, he was getting on our nerves. Trying to be funny, and perhaps to stir a reaction, he started leaving trash at our booth: lunch remains, empty mushroom boxes, and the like. At first, we simply returned the items. But when his behavior continued, we decided enough was enough. One evening, Natalie and I discussed our strategy: We could leave our trash at his booth—no, that might just provoke him. We could ask him to stop—but we'd already tried that. We could quit talking to him—that would be a shame because for the most part, he was friendly and fun, and we enjoyed interacting with him.

Natalie came up with the solution. Out came colored pencils and paper, and she set to work. First, she drew a wonderful rendition of Oscar the Grouch, with his furry head rising out of a battered trash can, the lid dangling off his head. His face expressed discontent. Next to Oscar, she drew a table adorned with granola bags, with a pile of trash next to them. Then she drew a dialogue box. In it, she wrote, "We are your neebors but we are NOT your trash can! And we don't want your trash at our booth!" At the bottom of the card, she wrote, "Thank you. Love, Natalie and Fiona."

The following Saturday, Natalie presented Chad with his card. She walked to his booth, handed it to him, and returned to our booth, no words spoken. We watched as he read it. He smiled, set the card down, and looked over at us. With a sheepish grin, he said, "Sorry, guys, I won't leave my trash in your booth anymore. I was just trying to be funny." We thanked him for honoring our request. I was proud of Natalie for the mature solution she had crafted, all on her own. No nasty confrontation, no anger, no retaliation. A simple, heartfelt, creative illustration took care of the issue.

That year, as with each new season of farmers market, I wanted to offer a new product. My customers had come to expect it. "So," they would say on their first day back, "whatcha got new for us this season?" By that time, many more people had discovered an intolerance to gluten; others simply felt better when they didn't eat it. In some families, everyone went off it to support a member with a gluten restriction.

My attempts to create a gluten-free granola had not succeeded. Access to a reliable source of gluten-free oats was challenging, as was finding a substitute for barley, which gave the granola an important depth and flavor. If I couldn't kick out the world's best gluten-free granola—one I could attach my name to with pride—I simply wouldn't offer any. Buyers who wanted it could purchase versions other companies had created.

I was determined, however, to offer a new gluten-free product. I decided on energy bars. Since the only possible gluten came from the oats, all we needed was a gluten-free substitute. One day, on a hike, the solution came to me: quinoa flakes! Since we used them for the Quinoa Crunch, we already had them in inventory. "This should be really easy!" I thought. "I'll just substitute quinoa flakes for the oats, and create new flavors. Shouldn't take long."

The granola bars were selling well. Chocolate Chip Peanut Butter was the most popular, followed by Cranberry Orange, Magical Mocha, and Tropical Spice. I set to work developing flavors similar to the current offerings but different enough to be distinctive.

Quinoa flakes are much more delicate than oat flakes. They are thinner and smaller and do not impart the same flavor—they have a straw-like taste, earthy and somewhat bitter. Because of their delicate nature, quinoa flakes absorb flavors much more readily than do other grains.

Since the Chocolate Chip Peanut Butter bar was our best seller, I created its twin first. Because I felt the peanut butter's strong flavor would overwhelm the delicate taste of the quinoa, I used almond butter instead and created Almond Chocolate Chip.

The first quinoa bar was easy to create, and it was tasty and satisfying. For the second, I developed a citrus-flavored bar, Lemon Cranberry, to mimic its granola bar twin, the Orange Cranberry. Those bars were delicate and flavorful, and they gained a quick following.

Then I turned to chocolate. I thought back to a Chocolate Mint granola bar I had created during an attempt to expand our energy bar selection at farmers market. Fresh from the oven, they were manna from heaven: rich and chocolate-y, with a bright flavor of peppermint. Unfortunately, those bars turned funky within just a few months. Since I had to guarantee a nine-month shelf life to get our products into distribution, that was problematic. Even if we only sold them at market and via the website, I worried the mint oil would turn before the bar was consumed. I took them out of production.

The next bar I'd created was Cherry Chocolate, which had been Natalie's inspiration. One night at dinner, she'd said, "You know, Mom, I wish you'd make a bar that's all chocolate but doesn't have coffee in it. That Magical Mocha bar is okay for adults, but kids don't like coffee." Although that had never occurred to me, she had a good point. I asked what flavor she'd like it to have.

"I don't know, maybe some kind of fruit." We discussed possibilities—cranberries, blueberries, raspberries—but nixed each idea for one reason or another. Suddenly her face lit up. "I know! How about cherries?" Cherries and chocolate? How could *anything* be wrong with that?

I set to the task. To give the base a cherry flavor, I sourced cherry concentrate, basically a very thick version of cherry juice. We also added dried cherries to the batter. Those Cherry Chocolate bars were fabulous—customers came to my booth just to buy them, normally by the caddy, fifteen at a time. But after a few months, because of rising ingredient costs, I discontinued them. The bars were already high-end, and I didn't want to charge more. I hated to disappoint my daughter, and my customers, but the tiny profit margin made that a necessary business decision.

When it came to the creation of a chocolate quinoa bar, at least I knew what *not* to do: no mint and no cherries. Since I liked the idea of a fruit and chocolate combination, I developed an orange chocolate bar instead, using orange oil; it turned out great. Moist and flavorful, the citrus was a nice complement to the chocolate. I named the bar Mandarin Chocolate. It sounded a bit exotic, and mandarins are a type of orange, after all.

I decided to create a tagline for the new bars. After researching the health benefits of quinoa, I learned that it is one of nature's few complete vegetarian proteins. A complete protein (also called a perfect protein) is one that contains all nine essential amino acids. One day on a hike it came to me: "A Complete Protein . . . A Complete Snack!"

Because of the ingredient costs, the profit margin for the quinoa bars was considerably lower than the granola bars. Still, I was happy with the new creations and introduced them that season. They were popular with customers, even those that could tolerate gluten. Our top seller was Almond Chocolate Chip, followed by Lemon Cranberry and Mandarin Chocolate. I brought them to Whole Foods, and Spice entered them into the system as a product line extension.

One Saturday at farmers market, the head chef of Brasserie, a downtown bistro, stopped by. The Orange Crunch granola was quite popular as a brunch item there. "Hi, Fiona!" he said. "How are things? Do you have any new products these days?"

"I do!" I replied, and showed him the quinoa bars. "They're pretty much like the granola bars, only they're made with quinoa, and they're gluten free."

He read the ingredients. "These sound really good," he said. "May I take a few samples back to the restaurant to see what the others think? We're revamping our menu, and maybe we can work these in somehow." I gave him a few samples, and he went on his way.

The following week, my phone rang. "Fiona, it's Tony from Brasserie. Everyone in here loves these quinoa bars! We'd like to pair the Lemon Cranberry with an assortment of French cheese and offer it as an appetizer platter. What do you think?"

I told him it sounded delicious, and that I'd never have thought to pair them with cheese. They purchased the bars by the sheet tray and cut them into triangles. The bar-and-cheese platter was offered at Happy Hour and turned out to be a popular menu item. The restaurant was one of my favorites, and it was fun to see my bars on the menu.

Although I hadn't consulted with Joanne to formulate the quinoa bars, I knew that had it not been for her creation of the granola bars, I wouldn't have had a prototype recipe to use. "Hey Joanne," I called and told her, "I've created a new line of energy bars. I don't need help with anything, but I think it's only fair to pay you a royalty, since I based the new bars on your original granola bar recipes." Joanne liked them but thought she could make minor improvements. We agreed that if I ever wanted to reformulate them, I would consult with her. We settled on a small royalty.

Our packaging—for both the individual bars and the caddies—was still bare-bones, and I knew it would have to be better if they were going to get into wider distribution. We were burning through money so quickly that the thought of another major expense made me cringe. But the bars were so good and doing so well that I knew they had the potential to gain a wider audience. My goal was to take them national.

Right about that time, I went with Natalie to a gluten-free symposium at the Copper Mountain ski resort in Colorado. In addition to all the sampling, I thought she might enjoy some of the seminars.

During one of the sessions, I sat next to Christy, a graphic designer who was pursuing a new career in holistic nutrition. She was fun and personable, and I liked her from the get-go. I shared my idea of repackaging our energy bars. She was eager to be involved in the natural food industry while supporting her career transition, and agreed to design the packaging.

While she worked on the designs, I wrote the copy. In addition to the earlier bar taglines, we included two new ones that came to me on a hike: "They're as different as they are delicious!" and "Energy . . . wrapped inside a bar!"

We listed the most important health benefits: Vegan, Rich in Omega 3, High in Fiber, and either Gluten Free or Wheat Free. We came up with a nutrition message for the top panel: Whole Food ~ Whole Body ~ Whole Mind ~ Whole Spirit to convey our belief that the foods we eat are intricately linked to how we feel in our bodies, minds, and spirits.

The crossover use of the "Organic Goodness in Every Bite!" tagline offered continuity to my product line—the bars were approximately

60 percent organic. To continue the tradition of quotes, I selected one for each bar.

Our bar caddy manufacturer was based in Denver. The owner purchased sufficient wind credits to offset production 100 percent, which said a lot—the facility was enormous, producing for companies such as Keebler, Nabisco, and Uncle Ben's. Thanks to the wind power usage, we included a little windmill logo with the wording, "Carton Made with Wind Energy." It added a nice touch.

Christy created caddy and film designs for six bars, and her talent shined through—the results were beautiful. Much of the message was communicated through the rich hues, curved lines, and earthy tones such as browns and rusts, golds and oranges, maroons and purples. A curved window in the bar wrapper showed off the bar inside. We designed the caddies to hold twelve bars, which is industry standard.

*   *   *

One of our bakers delivered to the coffee shop near our facility, where we sold our granola and energy bars. The owner, Stan, was friendly and sociable. He and his wife operated a second business in the space behind the shop: they packaged kites to sell to amusement parks.

One day, Stan received a bar delivery. "So, how do you guys package these anyway?" he asked. "Do you have a machine?"

My baker laughed. "Oh, no," he replied, "there is no machine. We cut the film by hand, slap on the labels, fill the sleeves, heat seal the ends, and affix the expiration date with a little price gun. It's a labor-intensive process."

"Well, I have an idea for you," Stan replied. He took my baker to the back of the facility. Lo and behold, right there in his warehouse, Stan had a horizontal packaging machine. Since they had recently liquidated their kite business, they no longer needed it.

When I learned of the machine, I was reluctant to see it. Looking around our facility, my eyes met dysfunctional equipment, broken-down parts, and tools that were not adequate to fix the problems.

"I know what you're thinking, Fiona," my baker said. "Yes, it's used and it does not come with a warranty. But Stan's a good guy, his shop is right here in the business park, and your products sell well for him. I don't think he would sell you a piece of junk. At least go look at it."

"Okaaay," I replied.

I walked through the business park to get there—I wanted fresh air, a clear head, and a positive an attitude before seeing yet another piece of used equipment.

Stan greeted me warmly. "Hi, Fiona! Good to see you. Come on back—I think you'll like what you see." When I set eyes on the flow wrapper, I almost cried. It was *exactly* what we needed, and the price was fair. Not only had he had meticulously maintained it, but he offered to haul it to the bakery, teach us to use it, and take it right back out if it didn't meet our needs. How could I turn that down? "Okay," I replied with a deep breath. "I'll take it. But only with a signed contract." He looked hurt, but after my earlier equipment debacles, which were intricately linked to men selling me machinery, I didn't plan to step into yet another deal with a handshake and closed eyes.

We set up the flow wrapper and had it running in record time. Of all the pieces of equipment, it was one of the most reliable. We experienced minor problems, but for the most part, it was efficient, dependable, and a huge time saver.

*   *   *

The day that Natalie and I drove to the symposium at Copper Mountain, my car was not happy. I had noticed something different with the transmission, as if the engine were barely functioning. The gears shifted okay, but I had to push the gas pedal harder than normal, and I smelled oil burning. The car chugged up the mountain roads, but with considerable effort. And the red engine light was on, which couldn't be good. I knew that what was happening was most likely my fault. Over the years, my car maintenance routine, which had once been very good, had fallen into oblivion. That was coming back to bite me.

We pulled up just a few minutes before one of the seminars was to start. I turned off the motor and got out of the car.

"What is that *horrible* smell?" I thought. I looked around, but instead of finding some other source, I realized it was coming from my own car. Then I saw black smoke pouring out from under the hood. I touched it—to my great dismay, it was hot. "Well, no time to deal with it now," I decided. "Hopefully, it will cool down by the end of the day."

"Mom," Natalie asked quietly as I helped her out of the car, "what's that horrible smell? And why is black smoke coming out of our car?" I told her I had no idea but was sure it would be okay by the time we left. She didn't look convinced. She glanced at me suspiciously but didn't say anything. The displeased look on my face must have told her it was best to not ask any more questions.

The symposium was action packed, and the hours flew by. I learned a lot about gluten-free baking. Natalie attending three classes with me and spent the rest of the day reading and coloring. My head was spinning when I collected our belongings and we headed out.

As we approached the car, Natalie said, "Mom, do you think Roo has cooled down by now?" We had named our car "Roo the Subaru," based on Winnie the Pooh.

"Oh, I'm sure it has, honey. Look how cold it is out. Roo can't possibly still be hot." But as much as I pretended not to look worried, I was quite concerned. We had an hour-and-a-half drive back to Boulder in the dark and cold. At least we'd mostly be going downhill, so I figured we could coast a lot if it came to that.

When I started the car, the red engine light went on. "Not again," I sighed. But the car started just fine, and I had no trouble shifting or braking. The smell was still there but not nearly as strong as it had been. Somehow, we got home safely.

I called a Subaru dealership the next day. "The red engine light won't go off," I explained. "Smoke has been pouring out the hood, and it smells something awful. I'm kinda worried."

"You should be worried," came the curt reply. "Better get it in here as early as possible tomorrow. And only drive it if absolutely necessary." After dropping Natalie off at school, I headed to the dealership. One of the mechanics did a quick assessment, shook his head, and let out a long, low whistle. "It's amazing you could drive it over here," he said. "But don't expect to be driving it out any time soon. This baby needs a complete overhaul."

"A complete *what*?" I asked. "Certainly it can't be that bad."

"Oh, it's that bad, all right. We're gonna have to rebuild this entire engine. You might get it back in a week, at the earliest."

I let out a huge sigh—this was going to set me back, for sure. The mechanic acknowledged my dismay. "Don't worry," he said. "We're gonna set you up with some nice wheels to tide you over. And by the time you get this baby back, you'll more or less have a brand-new car."

True to the mechanic's word, the dealership lent us a beautiful replacement, a new SUV with only twenty miles on it. I felt like a millionaire driving it around. Natalie was also impressed. "Wow, Mom!" she exclaimed when I picked her up from school. "Is this our new car? It's so fancy!"

I told her I also liked it but that we could only drive it until we got Roo back. "Oh," she said, a bit dismayed. We both enjoyed sitting high above the ground, and the ride was very comfortable. The SUV had more bells and whistles than I'd ever seen in a car. To my surprise, at the end of the week, Natalie told she me was ready to get Roo back.

"Really, honey?" I asked her. "Why is that? I thought you liked this car."

"I do like this car," she explained, "but I have to sit so far back. I like being closer to you. It's easier to pass stuff back and forth."

The dealership called the following week. "Your car is ready!" a friendly voice said. "We think you'll be pleased." When I went in, the mechanics were beaming. "Missy," one of them said, "you're looking at a brand-new engine. We also replaced the oil holding tank, and the oil filter. The entire mechanism was a disaster. To tell you the truth, we've never seen such a messed-up engine. It's amazing you could drive this thing around. When was the last time you brought it in for a maintenance check, or had the oil changed?" I admitted it had been quite a while. "Well, please don't let so much time go by from here on out," he replied. "I don't think you'll want to deal with this kind of repair again."

He wasn't joking. That engine replacement cost five thousand dollars. I gasped when I saw the bill. "Five thousand dollars! Surely it can't be that expensive." The invoice was neatly itemized, and he explained it line by line. Every repair, and every replaced part. But it was the labor cost that nearly made my eyes pop out, more than the engine and the new parts combined. There was no recourse, though. The damage had been done, due to my own neglect, and I had to pay for it. I took a deep breath and handed him my credit card, consoling myself with thoughts of all the airline miles I'd see on my next statement.

The mechanic walked me to my car, freshly washed and sparkling in the morning sun. "By the way," he said. "We were talking about your license plate. You must really like granola!"

"Yeah," I replied a little sullenly. I was in no mood to explain the plate. "I guess I do like granola."

I arrived to the office late that day. Rick didn't hide his sense of superiority about my automotive ordeals. He explained that he brought his car in for an oil change every five thousand miles, and had never missed a routine service.

"Good for you," I told him. I went into my office and firmly shut the door. I had no energy to hear more about car maintenance that day.

After all my years of being a responsible car owner, how could I have let this happen? The answer was obvious: Other priorities had taken over, and they didn't allow me the luxury to think about anything that wasn't urgent. My car had been running just fine, so it hadn't occurred to me that problems might be brewing under the hood. I didn't have a partner in my life to assume responsibility for car maintenance, and I certainly couldn't expect Natalie to keep me on the straight and narrow about automotive health. The norm was that I filled Roo with gasoline and window washer fluid, and that was the extent of our "maintenance."

I didn't have the money in my personal account to pay the bill. I'd have to take it from the business's bank account, probably by paying myself a distribution. But I let that burden go. With equipment costs and build-out expenses continually drawing down the account, what was another $5,000?

~14~
A BANK NOT TO BANK ON

"Tread softly! All the Earth is holy ground."
—English poet Christina Rossetti
(Quote on caddies of Lemon Cranberry Quinoa Bars)

Before the move, sales revenue covered our expenses with a good amount remaining, most of which I put into the business's bank account. My goal was to keep a healthy buffer; the company's financial stability stayed foremost in my mind.

After the move, cash flow began to move in the opposite direction. Although I continually made efforts to ensure the financial health of Fiona's Natural Foods, the company bank account was drifting toward the red, and quickly.

Our loan agreement required us to send the bank our monthly balance sheet and profit-and-loss statement. My original loan officers, Don and Shelly, were no longer in the picture. Several months after we had secured our funding, they both accepted a position at a different bank. I was dealing with new officers who were much less friendly, and at times impersonal. They saw me as a risky client full of liability rather than a local entrepreneur with superior products and far-reaching potential. They didn't know me personally, had probably never eaten my granola, and had only one concern: that I pay the note each month.

Secretly, I was more worried than they were—I had a lot on the line. In addition to my condo, I had listed pretty much everything else I owned as collateral. Fortunately, if I had to sell the condo, there was enough equity to pay off the loan. That was the last thing I intended to do, but I prepared myself emotionally for the possibility. To disrupt the comfortable home Natalie and I shared, one we had turned into a cozy space, would be almost unbearable for me. Our lifestyle would be interrupted, as well as the routine we had nicely fallen into after I started the company.

I was angry at myself for taking out such a large loan. I'd been raised by a father who made sure we lived sensibly and didn't spend more than we could afford. I had never been in debt, except for home mortgages, and I consistently paid off my credit card each month. I had never lived beyond my means, and as the owner of Fiona's, I had done my best to follow these same guidelines.

Borrowing such a large amount contradicted everything my father had taught us about debt avoidance and sensible money management. As much as I longed to reverse the clock and do things differently, the deed was done—all I could do was live it out. To ease my anxiety, I reminded myself what the other option had been. Going the investor route to grow the business would have meant giving up control of my company. I didn't mind the loss of equity as much as the loss of creative freedom and decision-making power. I also cherished the autonomy of making each day my own—I did not want to conform to someone else's guidelines or disrupt my schedule with Natalie. These were the reasons the bank loan had made sense.

One day, I was working from home when the doorbell rang. I wasn't expecting anyone and thought it must be a solicitor. When I opened the door, instead of finding a salesperson, I discovered one of the bank officers. He'd looked up the address on the loan paperwork and found my condo. Flustered, I asked about the purpose of his visit. I hadn't missed a payment or even made a late one. After we sat down, he told me the bank's loan officers had been going over our financials, and didn't have confidence I'd be able to pay off the loan—so they were withdrawing it. Somehow, I had to find a way to pay it off immediately. I could barely believe what I was hearing.

"But I've never missed a payment!" I exclaimed. To which he replied, "Yes, but if things keep heading in the direction they are now, you soon will. And we can't afford to take that chance."

He simply stared at me, and I tried to hold myself together. "But how am I supposed to pay off the loan immediately?" I asked. "Almost the entire amount is still due."

"Well," he replied, "this condo will get you what you need. Or you can sell the equipment. Since most of it is new, you might be able to get your money back and repay the loan that way."

I simply stared at him—dumbfounded, confused, and mortified. How could he do this to me, and in this manner? The man acted like a robot, not human at all, a robot who'd marched into my house with his file of documents and numbers. "I guess your other option is to secure another loan," he said. "Then you can pay us off and owe to another bank. But with these financials, good luck."

I was speechless and felt myself go numb. I just sat there, not knowing what to think or do. His job finished, he told me to consider my options and tell him my decision. Then he let himself out.

I was so utterly stunned, I couldn't move. My mind went blank. I sat motionless, staring at the room around me. Suddenly, I felt angry— but much more than that: I felt raging mad. I stood up and started screaming. "Why *me*, Goddammit! Why is this happening to *me*? Have I been such a bad person? Haven't I been working my *ass* off to keep this company going? And for what? For *this*? To lose my condo, or the means to make my granola?" I ranted and raved, but my anger wouldn't subside. "I should never have agreed to that stupid loan! Now what am I going to do?" I started crying, uncontrollably, inconsolably. I wanted to disappear—I didn't care where or for how long— to just go away, and when I returned, this whole nightmare would be over. Jouey, our little dog, scurried off to the bedroom. He was thirteen, arthritic, hard of hearing, and had lost some of his eyesight. But like all dogs, he was sensitive and perceptive. He knew something was terribly wrong and that I was terribly upset. He didn't want to be caught in the middle of it.

I'm an Irish redhead, from my mom's side. Like others in the family, when we get angry, we get *really* angry. Needing to take out my fury on something, I looked around. I didn't just need to *throw* something, I needed to *break* something. The condo was small, and most things there we used on a regular basis. I stormed down to the garage, which we used for storage. After a brief search, I laid my eyes on the perfect object: an old Mac computer I'd planned to donate to a local school.

So much for charity—I was in crisis. I hauled the computer upstairs, along with a heavy hammer. Then I closed my windows and blinds. The last thing I needed was a neighbor who reported to the police that I had gone out of my mind—even though perhaps I had done just that.

The venting began. I beat up on that computer until I couldn't see straight, hammering and banging and yelling and screaming profanities the entire time. I smashed that computer to bits, as hard as I could, as violently as I knew how. Among the tears and rage, I cursed at myself for being stupid and gullible. I cursed at Rick for convincing me to max out the loan and make such expensive purchases. I cursed at the bank for approving the loan to begin with, and then for sending an officer to my house to demand an early payoff.

I don't know how long I beat up on that computer, but when I stopped and looked around, metal and plastic bits graced every nook and crevice of my living room. I felt better, though. I had vented, and could breathe more easily again. As my heart rate returned to normal, exhaustion set in—physical, mental, and emotional. I couldn't focus, so I sat down, closed my eyes, and took deep breaths. Although I knew I had to do something, the solution—whatever it would be—could wait.

Fortunately, Natalie wasn't with me that night. I had plenty of time to clean up the condo and destroy all evidence of my anger episode. As I tidied up, I tried to stay calm and keep a clear head; perhaps a viable solution would come in. I had most of the next day to recuperate. Natalie was about to spend five nights with me; I was determined to pull myself together and act as if everything were fine. She was only eight years old; these were adult problems, and I wanted to protect her from them.

When I picked her up the next day, I did my best to behave as if the events of the previous twenty-four hours had not occurred. By the time we got home, though, she could tell I wasn't okay. "Mom, what's wrong?" she asked. "You're not acting right."

I took a deep breath, wondering what to say. How could I tell her what had happened? I didn't want her to worry. But I was a horrible liar, and was rarely able to conceal my emotions. With my exhale came the realization that I couldn't keep this from her. I sat her down and told it straight. I recounted the story: how the business wasn't doing so well, how the bank man had come over to say we needed to pay off our loan, and how I hadn't figured out how to do that as fast as he wanted. She looked at me intently, taking it all in.

I told her that if we couldn't quickly find a way to sell more granola, or find a different bank to lend us money, we might have to sell the condo. We would be fine, I told her, and I believed it. Selling the condo would net a hundred thousand dollars; the equipment would bring a hundred fifty thousand. The bank loan was just under a hundred eighty thousand. We would easily have enough money to live on while I looked for other work. With my master's degree in Spanish, together with teaching, writing, and social work experience, I was employable. I would lose the equity in the condo, but we would have a roof over our heads. That much I had thought through before I picked her up that afternoon.

I asked Natalie not to worry. No matter what, I told her, we would be fine—the worst that might happen is we would have to move. I also told her I was doing everything I could to figure it out. Though my explanation was brief, it was detailed enough for her to understand. I took a deep breath and gave her a hug, both to comfort me and to reassure her. Somehow I managed to block my tears, and we went about the rest of our evening together. She never cried, and she seemed to believe me when I told her we'd be okay.

Later that evening, she got ready for bed. After brushing her teeth, she selected her clothes for the next day and put on her jammies. Afterward, she was reading in bed while I worked downstairs. I missed the joy of reading together as we had done when she was younger, but by this age, she had outgrown that.

Just as I was about to go tell her it was time for lights out, she suddenly appeared at the table. In one hand she held a slip of paper. She looked at me intently, then passed me the note, which she had neatly folded.

"Don't read this till I'm in bed asleep," she said. I thanked her for the note and promised I would wait to read it. In her other hand was a little bag which she set on the table and told me not to open until after I'd read the note. I agreed, then tucked her into bed and waited as patiently as possible until she fell asleep. She dozed off quickly. With much anticipation, I unfolded the note. The front side said:

> Do not look
> on other
> side till
> bedtime.
> —Natalie
> Do not give back!!!!!!!

Then I cheated. I couldn't wait that long to read the other side. I took a breath and slowly turned it over. The back said:

> Do not give back.
> $33.78
> Love Natalie
> Split it up between the
> company and personal.

With a bit of hesitation, I reached for the bag. Inside, I discovered every last penny she owned. She had been saving her money, but now, after learning about our situation, had decided to give it all to me. The stream of tears began, and didn't stop for a long time. I just wanted to crawl into her bed and hold her. Sweet, tender Natalie. Still so young yet very much exposed to unpleasant, adult life "stuff." Though I shielded her as best I could from the difficult circumstances in my life, some things couldn't be hidden, and this was one of them.

I cried myself to sleep that night. In the morning, I went to Natalie's room and woke her with a huge hug. I held her in my arms, and the tears started all over again. She asked why I was sad. I told her I couldn't accept the money, that it was hers, and that we would be okay without it.

She pulled away and said, "No, Mom, that is *your* money now. I won't take it back. And you have to promise me you'll spend it half on yourself and half on the business." I continued to hold her, until she started squirming. I realized this came from her heart, and it was what she wanted. I took a deep breath and said, "Okay, I'll keep the money. And I'll spend it how you want. Thank you, honey. I love you so much." She gave me a bright smile, a warm hug, and a friendly kiss on the cheek. Then we carried on with our morning.

*   *   *

A few days after the bomb fell, it occurred to me to let Don know what had happened at his former bank. Surprised and disturbed, he said he'd try to help. Somehow, he worked his magic with the new bank. I was offered a new loan which not only paid off the original note but the interest rate also was a quarter of a percentage point less. At least something good had come from all that torment. Don assured me that he and Shelly had every confidence in my business's success.

In addition to our bank loan, Rick had convinced me to obtain a second company credit card, which came with a thirty-thousand-dollar line of credit. He assured me we would use it only for emergencies and incidentals, so that if something came up unexpectedly, we'd have a line of credit to cover it. The new card got maxed out quickly—and the debt with its line of credit came with a hefty interest rate.

The strain of being underneath so much debt weighed on my psyche. Like hot, heavy metal, stress poured itself into the depths of my core and settled there. Heaviness engulfed me, exhaustion numbed me, and regret consumed me. Even my colorful office—bright, sunny, and plastered with Natalie's adorable artwork—no longer felt cheerful. As the months progressed, those warm orange walls emanated a sense of doom and despair. The entire bakery—once filled with hope and promise and potential—become saturated instead with a sense of foreboding. My health, which I had tried hard to maintain, deteriorated on all levels. My life became a grueling, swirling, chaotic mess. And stirred into that toxic brew was the heavy responsibility that somehow, I needed to find a solution—before it was too late.

~15~

EXPANSION AND CONTRACTION

"Ineffable grace is ever present."
—Anonymous
(Quote on boxes of Strawberry Mango Quinoa Crunch)

When the cereal boxes arrived, they were stunning. As I sat on my office floor and opened a case of each variety, a bright rainbow spread forth, engulfing me in vivid hues. The royal blue logo was surrounded by earth tones: orange, violet, rose, cinnamon, teal, gold, red, purple, brown, fuchsia. I was washed over by emotion, and tears streamed forth. Here they were, my beautiful boxes. These would be my tickets out of this mess, one-way tickets that would journey to new places, grace supermarket shelves, and send revenue back my way in return. I felt light and hopeful for the first time in a long time.

Whole Foods kept its promise. Scott set me up with a UNFI buyer who guided me through the paperwork. I agreed to pay for new insurance policies, returns, quarterly advertisements and promotions, and free fill. The free fill almost killed me. In my quest to be a respectable steward of the planet, I had chosen to produce cases with twelve boxes of cereal, while other granola companies packaged six to a case. The result of my efforts to save a tree and a little tape meant that every Whole Foods store in the region received twelve boxes of ten varieties free—a hundred twenty boxes of cereal for each store. Not only was this completely idiotic on my part, but the stores didn't like it either. Whole Foods had added the entire line of cereal to the regional schematic, which meant each store made room for ten new cereal facings. But since only eight boxes fit from front to back, they had to store the extras as back stock. That did not make the grocery guys happy. Warehouse space is hot real estate and not given up lightly. Had the stores received six boxes per case, they could have ordered when each variety was down to two and fit the entire new case behind the existing boxes. Why I didn't just cut my losses with the twelve-pack boxes and switch to six-pack boxes, will remain a mystery. My brain at that point was more or less mush, resulting in some very costly business decisions.

Overnight, Fiona's Granola was in twenty-five Whole Foods markets. And the region was expanding. With ten cereal varieties in each store, sales had the potential to liberate us from our negative cash flow. Some of the new revenue, though, was already spoken for. In addition to the initial distribution requirements, another cost was demos: at least one three-hour demo per store, each quarter. That was a hundred demos a year, just for Whole Foods. Since it was important to have personal contact with customers and store employees, and make sure all the varieties were stocked, we preferred to do the demos ourselves. This was easy enough in Colorado and New Mexico, but for accounts elsewhere, paying store personnel to conduct the demos seemed like our only alternative.

One day, out of the blue, Rick offered to do a demo at each of the twenty stores in Texas. He would drive his own car and camp most of the time, helping keep our demo budget to a minimum. His costs would certainly be cheaper than paying for the demos, and since our funds were diminishing quickly, I readily agreed.

While Rick was on the road, my parents came to visit. Together with my brother-in-law Dave, who had been involved in startups, we strategized about minimizing expenses and becoming profitable again. But when Rick came back, he didn't appreciate our having discussed the company's finances without him.

The morning after he returned, I was out walking Jouey when my phone rang. It was Rick, calling to resign. I hadn't expected this, and could barely comprehend the significance. Was it possible the relationship could end so abruptly? Just like that? He said he had sent me a resignation email and would gather his belongings when my family was not at the bakery.

Although our opinions often differed, causing stress between us, the thought of running the company myself almost paralyzed me. Suddenly I would have to take over the tasks he'd been doing on top of everything already on my own plate. Somehow, I told myself, I would find a way. Upon hearing the news, my parents and brother-in-law were equally shocked, but they assured me I would get through the transition and figure out a plan to move forward.

One evening the following week, I was alone at the bakery when Rick walked in, unannounced. He collected his items and returned his key. Our words were few but cordial.

As soon as he was gone, I burst out in tears. I cried because I was relieved. I cried because of the stress. I cried because I was completely exhausted. I cried because I had no idea if I could save my company. I cried because of all the sacrifices I'd made, and for the way my health had deteriorated. I cried for being a complete idiot and not seeing the situation as it really was. I cried for the rose-colored glasses I'd put on which totally distorted my world. Finally, I cried because of the affect my stress was having on Natalie, no matter how hard I tried to hide it from her.

The tears did not stop gushing, for a long time. My sorrow was followed by shame—shame that I hadn't shared my difficulties with others, shame that I had not asked for help, shame that I'd allowed good employees to leave, shame that I hadn't followed good advice, shame that I hadn't changed the situation, and shame that I had kept friends and loved ones in the dark, simply because I was too embarrassed to share my worries with them. Finally, I felt shame that I had faltered in my duties as a mother.

I'd missed most of Natalie's soccer games. I'd delivered her late to birthday parties and other events. I hadn't planned many playdates or invited her friends over. Worse than those things, I had never spent an entire day at school with her, though she'd been asking me since the first grade. Now she was in the third.

"Please, Mommy," she'd say. "Won't you spend a whole day at school with me? It will be so fun!" I wanted to, so badly. Yet, somehow, I had never managed to carve out just one entire day to spend at school with my daughter. Always too busy, always too much work. That night, I felt like a complete failure. I had failed my family, I had failed my company, and I had failed myself. And for what? What good could possibly come from all that pain? Only a complete fool or someone totally out of her mind would attempt to run her life the way I had. That night, with all those tears shed, I wasn't sure I had the strength to move my life in a better direction.

~16~
When Less Can Be More

"One who would travel happily must travel lightly."
—Antoine de Saint-Exupery
(Quote on boxes of Cinnamon Spice Granola)

Through all the darkness, Natalie's boundless creativity and sweet personality were shafts of light that brightened my days and brought much-needed sunshine into my life. One day when I picked her up from school, she handed me a card. "Oh, what's this?" I asked. She beamed and said, "It's something I made for you today." She had taken a large piece of pink construction paper and made a Mother's Day card. On the front was a colorful drawing of girls and boys playing together. Inside were "The Top 10 Reasons Why I Love My MOM." Each sentence was partially complete but ended with a blank line, which the kids filled in. Natalie's list read:

10. I love my Mom because she reads me <u>Alice in Wonderland</u>.
9. I love my Mom because she helps me <u>decide what to wear</u>.
8. I love my Mom when she makes me laugh by <u>tickling me</u>.
7. I love my Mom because she taught me how to <u>climb a structure</u>.
6. I love to hear my Mom sing "<u>Zippety-do-dah</u>."
5. I love my Mom because she finds time to <u>play with me</u>.
4. I know my Mom cares because she <u>buys me games</u>.
3. I know my Mom is smart because she <u>makes granola</u>.
2. I love my Mom because she works so hard at <u>the kitchen</u>.
1. I love my Mom because she's the BEST MOM EVER!

Tears came to my eyes. Maybe I wasn't doing so poorly in the motherhood department after all. At least I knew I was doing the best I could.

Ongoing testimonials were the other rays of light that nudged me forward. They reminded me that my efforts were appreciated beyond what I could see in my day-to-day life. A woman stopped by market. "We talk to you from our bedroom," she said. "In the middle of the night I say, 'Honey, Fiona's calling!' And I get up and eat a bowl of your granola. This is the best stuff on earth." Another woman saw me at Whole Foods. "I have never tasted granola this good in all my life!" she exclaimed. "And I'm a child from the '60s— so this is my kind of food." Another told me the granola was her favorite splurge food. "I'm telling you girl—you've got a product that is fabulous. I love it like a good album. I hope you make lots of money because you've worked your butt off." One man said, "When I first met you, I felt like I was meeting a rock star."

Other kinds of recognition came by accident. One day, an employee came over. She was noticeably excited. "Fiona, you're never going to believe this!" She handed me the latest edition of *Men's Journal*. Inside was an article about the benefits of a plant-based diet, which featured an interview with the co-founder of Twitter, Biz Stone, who had gone vegan. When asked about breakfast, he was quoted as saying, "I eat maybe a half-cup of Fiona's All Natural Granola, the Organic Ginger Walnut flavor, and a splash of rice milk." I almost fell out of my chair. The co-founder of Twitter, eating *my* granola? How he'd found it and continued to purchase it was beyond me, as my products were not in distribution in his part of the country.

One year I traveled to Utah, where my brother and sister-in-law lived, to demo at the Whole Food stores. They joined me for the demo in Park City. Afterward, we drove to Sundance. After strolling the grounds, we went inside the cafe. What I saw on the opposite side of the room made me cry out in delight. Right there, on a hand-crafted shelf all to themselves, were Fiona's Granola boxes. We looked at each other, and my brother said, "Is that cool or *what?*" After the cereals were in distribution, they traveled to many locations serviced by UNFI, many of which were unknown to me. The fact they were at Sundance made me smile. I had always been a Robert Redford fan—the thought that he probably ate my granola made my heart skip a beat.

*   *   *

After poring over the books with my family, one thing was clear: I needed to cut expenses—Big Time. The rent was simply too high for our revenue. I would have to either downsize or bring other companies into the bakery. Sharing the equipment didn't appeal to me, since increased use and changes in settings would probably result in frequent repairs. Could I trust others to use the equipment correctly, be respectful, clean up after themselves, stick to their time slots, and pay the rent on time? Configuring the space to meet the needs of others seemed daunting and would require energy that would be difficult for me to muster. Moreover, after all I had been through, the thought of more risk unnerved me.

My parents had suggested that I talk with Steve. He was approachable, fair, and showed a genuine interest in my company. The cards were in his favor, since our lease guaranteed he would recoup his investment in the build-out. He was a smart businessman, so perhaps he could figure out a way for the situation to work for both of us.

I summoned the courage to call him, and we set up a meeting. Fighting back tears, I laid everything out for him. He learned what a mess the company was in financially, that revenue was not keeping up with expenses, that the books were in dire need of mending, and that I didn't see a way to keep going under the current circumstances. He understood the gravity of the situation. He knew about Natalie, and that my condo was on the line. He knew the bank would take the equipment, which would most likely put me out of business. He realized I might be forced to declare bankruptcy.

Steve heard me out. He could see that the amount of product leaving the bakery didn't justify the expenses of my loan, my rent, and the cost of the build-out. He took a long breath and smiled. His kind face released my tears. He said our meeting had come at an opportune time, and that he had an idea. The specialty hardware company next door was growing and looking to expand. The owners preferred to stay where they were but thought they'd have to move to a new building Steve had under way, since ours was fully occupied.

Steve suggested we downsize the bakery. He would make the necessary alterations in the building—at a cost to me of ten thousand dollars. When I asked about our rent, he said it would be reduced by 80 percent. *A rent reduction of 80 percent?* It seemed too good to be true—until I realized I'd be left with 20 percent of the space. He said he wished he didn't have to reduce the space so drastically, but the location of the support beams dictated where the wall could be built. I didn't think we could operate in such a tiny area, but he was convinced we could do it.

Steve became my hero. He stayed friendly and positive, never passed judgment, and helped me find a solution. He truly cared about me and my business. Also, it probably helped that he loved my granola and I gave him as much as he could eat. Some of it he took on his hiking adventures. Steve had summited some of the world's highest peaks, and he carried the granola with him to be eaten as a treat on the top.

Reducing our production area was a Band-Aid, and it would stop the bleeding. But, it would also make significant growth impossible. After all I had gone through, I wanted more than a Band-Aid. Exhausted or not, I was eager to see my company grow to its full potential. The next step was to finally bring in an investor, someone with experience in the food industry. I didn't have much to offer besides equity, but I was willing to liberally dish it out in hopes of growing the company.

I considered the investors who had approached me over the years. A man I'd known since my chamber of commerce days came to mind. He had a background in the wine industry and had managed various companies, most of them from the startup stage. After he told me he was involved in other ventures and no longer available, he suggested another potential investor we knew, named Leonard.

Leonard and I had a long chat. His background was in chemical engineering, but he'd been involved with manufacturing plants and knew equipment well. He had left corporate engineering to pursue his dream of building manufacturing plants off the grid, powered exclusively by photovoltaic cells. He had partners and potential funding.

What he needed was a prototype company that could test his plan and assess the new technology. The avid tree hugger in me loved the idea. By joining forces, we could do each other a favor and realize our dreams together. I also recognized a synchronistic grace in the whole idea, my father being a solar physicist and all.

Soon, Leonard and his wife were 15 percent owners of Fiona's Natural Foods. In addition to helping us move into the smaller space, Leonard helped negotiate the sale of the tunnel oven. Fortunately, I had found a buyer, a snack food manufacturer in Denver that was looking for just such an oven to make dog biscuits. Not only was that massive beast finally removed from my sight, but the revenue paid for the wall and the labor to downsize my production operations.

Leonard also loaned me $25,000 for more boxes, as we had already gone through the first run. I had created recipes for each cereal line, and for two cents a box more, I chose to print them on the inside, formatted to look like recipe cards. For the granola boxes: Berry Cobbler, Chocolate Chip Cookies, and Raspberry Granola Bars. For the muesli boxes: Apple Crumble, Mimi's Muesli Cake, and Harvest Cookies. And for the Quinoa Crunch boxes: Pan Seared Chicken, Fiona's Famous Stuffing, and Quinoa Cookies.

*   *   *

The downsizing was quick and efficient. The equipment fit, but barely. Our new space looked like a long alley. It was so narrow the forklift could barely make the 360-degree turn needed to load and unload pallets. We still had one dock door, which allowed fresh air and sunshine to enter.

I was mostly concerned about my new baker, Jared, who I had recently hired to replace my previous one, who had to quit because of a rotator cuff injury. Jared had just completed a program at Joanne's culinary school, and she praised him highly. Not only did he enjoy the small space, but he thrived in it. He loved working alone, which was a good thing, since soon after he started, I fired my part-time baker. In addition to health issues, the complexity of the packaging equip-

ment gave him troubles. Jared, with his steady focus and inherent culinary talents, did the work of both men. He learned to operate the
equipment in record time, and he figured out new production effi-
ciencies. He was fast, organized, reliable, competent, and friendly. His
joyful presence was much-needed medicine for my battered spirit. I
paid him more than I had ever paid another baker, and he was worth
every penny.

Jared got our products into a local shop in the eastern plains, where
he drove to regularly to purchase raw milk and local meat. When the
owner, Phil, learned about my company, he asked for samples. I happily loaded Jared up, and he passed them along on his next visit. Phil
loved the entire line and called the following day to order in each variety. The products sold surprisingly well in his store, even the quinoa
and muesli cereals, and he became a loyal customer. If he needed supplies before Jared returned, Phil drove in and picked them up.

Months passed, and sales were steady. UNFI and Sysco orders came
in like clockwork, and we easily filled them. People were amazed at
the amount of cereal and energy bars we moved out of that tiny space.
As icing on the cake, for the first time in a long time, revenue topped
expenses. I could feel myself breathe, and tension left my body. I once
again worked from home, which was much easier on my personal life.
I felt certain the worst was behind me.

Orders came in via my fax machine. Often, they arrived in the middle of the night. I was usually in a deep sleep when the three-ring tone
would suddenly wake me. During the day, I welcomed those rings. At
night, I cursed them. Then I usually went upstairs to see who had ordered and the dollar amount; I was often too elated to go back to sleep.

Fiona's Granola seemed to have a life of its own. Farmers market
sales increased our orders in other states, thanks to customers who
returned with my products and contacted local businesses to bring
them in. Coffee shops, yoga studios, restaurants, independent groceries, and B&Bs in faraway states placed orders. From Rainbow Grocery in San Francisco to high-end specialty shops in Manhattan, word
spread, as did demand. Harry, the "granola connoisseur" with a cafe
in upstate New York who had discovered my granola at the food co-

op early on, increased his orders, as did a cafe in New Jersey. The out-of-state businesses had to pay shipping on top of the cost of a premium product, but they didn't seem to mind.

Amazon added all the boxed cereals and energy bars in four warehouses across the country. To have a presence on such a widely used website was great exposure. But with Amazon's terms, it didn't add a lot to the bottom line. Amazon retained 23 percent: 13 for "Subscribe & Save," 2 for "damage," 3 for "freight allowance," and 5 for "EDLP "—Every Day Low Price. Although Amazon paid the freight and priced the products competitively, it was our discounts that made the low pricing possible.

Local organizations requested my products, and I strived to be generous. I donated granola and energy bars to school fundraisers, the homeless shelter, the women's safe house, congregations, health fairs, nonprofit organizations, athletic events, youth groups, radio stations, and charity groups. The publicity was good, and I enjoyed giving back to local communities.

*   *   *

I had known my tax accountant, Cindy, since childhood. Our fathers worked together at the solar observatory in Sunspot, New Mexico. Not only did we go through school together but we also shared the same house growing up. All the families in town lived in government housing, and there were only four styles. One was a duplex, which is where we lived, with Cindy's family on the other side. We were both the youngest of three kids. Her older sister, Becky, was the same age as my sister, Karen, and her older brother, Tony, was the same age as my brother, David. We were mirror families living on opposite sides of our adjoining wall. We rode the school bus together, played together, and shared an occasional overnight. I loved to go to Cindy's for breakfast because her mom cooked sausage with biscuits and gravy, which was never on the menu at our house. She loved to eat breakfast at our house because my mom made granola, which was not to be found on her side.

A year after we moved down the mountain from Sunspot to Alamogordo, her family made the same move and bought a house just a
few blocks away. Our lives continued to intertwine. One summer,
Cindy and I got jobs washing cars at a local dealership. New Mexico
summers are hot down in the desert, so it wasn't a bad way to spend
the summer. Not only could we could cool ourselves with the hoses,
but every so often we'd soak each other just for fun.

Cindy was cute as a button, with huge blue eyes and wavy blond
hair. She had a cute little figure too, which didn't hurt at the carwash. I
had a nice figure also, but the length of my shorts and style of my tops
were more reserved. Most important, she was a very hard worker. She
put her heart and soul into cleaning those cars. I was happy to rid them
of dirt and make them shine, but Cindy scrubbed and buffed them until
they gleamed like diamonds in the bright New Mexico sunshine.

One day, the managers of the car wash called Cindy into the office.
We looked at each other, wondering if she was about to get fired. If
so, I wondered why they weren't firing me instead, as she was by far
the better worker. When she got to the office, she was told something
like this: "Cindy, you're a real hard worker, and we'd like to reward
that. We have some administrative work that needs doing, along with
some light accounting, and we're simply not finding the time. If you'd
like to work in the office instead of wash cars, we can train you on the
accounting; the rest will explain itself." They also told her the pay
would be higher.

When Cindy returned to tell me, I couldn't help but feel happy for
her. But I was sad for myself at the same time. I would lose my companion. How much fun would it be washing cars alone all day long?
But that's the way I was left.

Cindy enjoyed the office work and was a natural with the accounting. She picked up the concepts easily and soon became the dealership's accountant. She continued working part-time during the school
year and full-time in the summers. After graduating, she went on to
take accounting courses, earn certifications, and become an enrolled
agent. Eventually she started her own accounting firm, which she manages to this day.

Our lives continued on parallel tracks. We both moved to Colorado and continued to see each other occasionally. She was the first person who came to mind when I needed an accountant for my business.

When she learned about my company, she was enthusiastic. "A granola company! That's so great!" she exclaimed. "You always made the best granola. Remember when I used to go to your house after school sometimes just to eat some?"

Because we lived an hour apart, monthly accounting was not practical. But Cindy agreed to become my company tax accountant.

The first two years, she mentioned how pleased she was with the company's success. At the end of year three, she said, "Wow, Fiona, you have literally doubled your sales each year. And you're on an upward trend. It's been really fun to see the business grow." She was delighted at the diversity of our accounts, which included engineering firms, boutique hotels, bike shops, chiropractic offices, the Boulder airport coffee shop, wilderness institutes, daycare dropoff centers, and even a little taquería in Denver. Some of my most loyal customers were members of Over the Arroyo Gang, a large group of outdoor enthusiasts based in Santa Fe.

* * *

When Rick left, the first order of business was to give the books a complete overhaul. I followed Cindy's suggestion and hired a bookkeeper with manufacturing company experience. Her name was Barb. She came highly recommended, and I suspected that if anyone could do what was needed, she was my gal. She wasted no time. On our first day together, after learning about the parting with Rick and how little money was left in the business account, she looked me square in the eye. "Fiona," she said, "I'm not gonna mince words. This is a mess, and it will take me a while to straighten things out. *But* we will get through it, and we'll get you back on track."

With those words, new tears gushed forth. Even with my new sense of levity, I was still raw. My tears didn't stop her. "I know we can do this," she said. "There's every reason to believe you can have a healthy company again." Barb let me cry, and vent a little. Then she told me it was time to get to work.

The first thing Barb did was to set up a "suspense account." I thought that was her name for expenditures we were "in suspense" about, but I learned these accounts are commonly set up to temporarily hold unclassified transactions while a decision is made as to their classification. For most companies, an entry in a suspense account can be either a debit or a credit, but in my case, all the "suspenseful transactions" were debits.

Barb and I dove into those expenditures with a vengeance. In one case, she found a check to one of my bakers that was not part of payroll. "What's this?" she asked. "Why would your baker just get some random check that has nothing to do with payroll? If he bought something for the business and you reimbursed him, it should be coded to whatever part of the business benefitted."

That expense had benefitted only Rick. I fessed up. "Yeah," I told her. "I remember that one. Rick bought some pot from David, and instead of paying with his own money, he wrote a company check." She looked at me, dumbstruck. I had only found out after the fact when David told me he wasn't pleased about getting a company check for an illegal transaction, especially since they had agreed on payment in cash. To avoid coding anything unlawful, the expenditure got parked in the suspense account and never came out.

Barb and I worked tirelessly, for weeks. She was a joy to be around; not only did I have utmost confidence in her ability to straighten things out, but a friendship blossomed between us. She was candid with me, and her detective work got to the bottom of most of the mysteries. With each passing day, I sensed a lightheartedness that had been missing from my life for a long time. A feeling of freedom came over me, and I felt sure I could once again take control of both my business affairs and my personal life. I breathed more easily, slept better, and my panic attacks went away.

Once we had the books in working order, we moved to monthly reconciliation. The first few months were rocky. As we went into each expense account to record new transactions, previous transactions appeared that didn't seem tied to anything specific. Through that painful but eye-opening process, I came to understand every expense and how to code it. Equally important, I understood exactly how much money was in the business's bank account, I had a good idea what my cash flow should look like, and I understood the extent of my debt. My accounting skills improved, thanks to Barb and the procedures she taught me. Before I knew it, the books were legible and made sense to both of us. The monthly accounting became routine and enjoyable. And the biggest gift of all? For the first time in a long time, I took control of the finances. It was an authority that empowered me and gave me confidence about my company and its well-being.

~17~
THE RECESSION SURVIVAL KIT

"It's good to have an end to journey toward,
but it is the journey that matters, in the end."
—Ursula K. Le Guin
(Quote on caddies of Chocolate Chip Peanut Butter Granola Bars)

Tighter control of spending helped our profits grow exponentially after Barb and I took control of the finances. In twelve months, the bank balance quadrupled—as if by magic. I was in continual shock as I opened my statements each month. I didn't pay attention to the details. Knowing the numbers were on the rise, and that Barb had a watchful eye on things, let me focus on the company's growth.

I put my energies back into sales and marketing. The next order of business was to get back into farmers market, as Rick had talked me out of participating the previous year so we could focus on large accounts instead. The move had not felt right to me, but I went along. Only time would tell if I could rectify that one.

I set off to market one bright, Saturday morning, toward the end of the season. I was a bit nervous, as slots for food vendors filled up quickly. The manager, Mark, seemed pleased to see me. I told him it had been a mistake to take the year off, and that I missed seeing my customers and the social aspects of market. "Fiona," he said, "there will always be a spot for you. We'd love to have you back." I was so relieved, tears welled up and I gave him a huge hug. He said it had taken months for people to stop saying, "Where's Fiona?" "What happened to Fiona?" "Market isn't the same without Fiona!" I had no idea I'd become such a fixture there, but knowing I was missed brought yet more tears to my eyes.

Market sales were strong, and Natalie was happy to spend her Saturdays there once again. The one advantage of our time off had been that for a full year, I could attend her games and call myself a soccer mom. She quit the year after we returned.

In my five years at market, I had never missed the opportunity to introduce a new product each season. I decided that year would be no different. I felt ready to branch out from cereals and energy bars. Although I was pleased that none of my products were very sweet, they were also not what one could call savory. I'm a snacker, and when I snack, I crave salty over sweet. I also like protein in my snacks. I thought about what I could offer in terms of a savory, protein-rich snack. I didn't have to ponder too long.

Being a nut fanatic, I decided roasted nuts would be the next product line. But not just any nuts. These would be flavored, roasted nuts like no others on the market. Although nuts were expensive, my audience cared about healthy eating and was willing to spend money for top-quality products. Not only would it be fun to create different flavors using different nuts, but since flavored nuts were hard to find, I also might be able to create a niche market. I went into creativity mode.

When I began sourcing ingredients, I asked my suppliers if they had ideas for alternative oils—I had been looking for an alternative to canola for quite awhile. One suggested rice bran oil; to my delight, it worked like a charm. It had a neutral flavor, could be heated to high temperatures, was shelf stable, had never been genetically modified, was readily available, and was only slightly more expensive than canola. I also tested it in the cereals and bars, and it worked like a dream. Finally, a viable solution! I decided to replace the canola with this new oil for all my products.

The new line was challenging, since a dedicated "artisan nut" category had not been created yet. Because there were very few flavored nuts on the market, retailers didn't know what to do with them. Nuts could be found in the bulk bin, but most were salted and roasted, or plain and raw. As for canned nuts, most were Planters peanuts. Since the product line would be new, I considered the field wide open. Jared liked the idea and said incorporating nuts into our production schedule wouldn't be a problem.

To get the creative juices flowing, off I went on a bike ride. That netted the first flavor: Chipotle Pecan. As a New Mexican, I make chile one of my first considerations in food creation. I love chile, no matter the color, variety, heat intensity, or how it's served. Over the years, chipotle had become my go-to chile. I knew that its smoky, robust flavor would lend itself well to combining with pecans, which I also love. They are a nut I also love, both for their flavor and because they can easily be incorporated into many food products, both sweet and savory. I had grown up eating pecans and chile but had never had the two together. I thought it could be a match made in heaven. A new challenge in front of me, I set out to create my first flavored nut.

First task: find chipotle powder. What my suppliers sent lacked the depth of flavor so characteristic of chipotle pepper, so I decided to see what Whole Foods had to offer. There, in the spice aisle, I found just the one. The crimson color was my first indication, and the place of origin—New Mexico—my second. The company, Los Chileros, was based in Albuquerque. Its chipotle was smokier and more robust than the varieties from my suppliers, and had the perfect amount of heat. I contacted the company and learned it would be happy to sell me the chile powder in ten-pound bags.

My recipes had always been clean and simple, and the nuts were no exception. I combined pecans, chipotle powder, sea salt, and a little oil to help the dry ingredients adhere to the nuts. That first batch of Chipotle Pecans turned out *perfect*. I was stoked and immediately became addicted.

Next idea: Curry Cashews. Because my suppliers' curries didn't offer the flavor I wanted, and my efforts to combine spices were unsuccessful, my first attempts failed. I could imagine the perfect flavor, but it eluded me.

One day, the owner of a local spice shop stopped by my booth at farmers market. I had known him since my chamber days. He asked how things were going, and I told him about my latest product line and my dilemma finding the right curry. I had tried his blends also, but they were either too sweet, not spicy enough, or not complex enough for the flavor profile I hoped to achieve. He thought a moment and said, "How about if I create a custom blend for you? Just tell me what you're after, and I'll blend a few samples."

I described my target flavor profile, and he called a few days later with three custom blends he'd created. After a few trial runs, based on what I liked and didn't like about each blend, he created a fourth. That was the best yet. I asked him to kick up the heat a notch, and he did, making a fifth variety that was perfect. We enjoyed creating the blend together, and I was happy to use a locally made spice. I kept the recipe simple: cashews, curry, sea salt, and oil.

I was having fun with the new product line and kept it going. The next flavor that came to me, on another bike ride, was Rosemary Hazelnuts. I ordered samples of dried rosemary sprigs and hazelnuts. Although visually appealing and bursting with flavor and texture, the sprigs did not adhere well to the nuts, even with the addition of oil. My supplier solved the dilemma. He suggested powdered rosemary, and it worked beautifully. It adhered to the nuts and enveloped them with a subtle green hue. But although the powder allowed the flavor to be distributed nicely, I missed the texture and visual appeal of the sprigs. In the end, I added both, in equal quantities.

After creating the savory varieties, I decided to try a sweet flavor. I was on a hike when the next idea came in: Walnuts à L'Orange. Two of my favorite products were the Orange Crunch granola and the Cranberry Orange granola bars, largely because of the flavor and aroma imparted by the orange oil. I had never heard of orange-flavored nuts but decided to give it a go. Agave was the easiest sweetener we had on hand to incorporate with the orange oil. To my delight, they were a dream. The orange oil gave the nuts a beautiful glaze, and the flavor combined well with that of the walnuts.

I was on a roll and wanted to keep it going. Since we had almonds in the bakery, I decided to use them to create something a bit more familiar to the average palate. Roasted cinnamon almonds are a staple at outdoor winter festivals. And because Cinnamon Almond granola was one of our most popular items, I knew my customers liked this flavor combination. I set to work.

Since the other nuts had gone well, I expected the same for this, my final creation. But that was wishful thinking. First, the almonds clumped up as if they were held together with molasses. When they finished baking, we were faced with a solid mass of sticky, gooey nuts. Even Jared—tall with strong, large hands—barely managed to break up the glutinous mass. Second, running the almonds through the packaging machine was a nightmare. They clogged the chute and left sticky residue inside. The procedure had to be abandoned, even though packaging by hand was a painstakingly slow, gooey mess which increased my labor cost.

We had two choices: abandon the recipe or revise it. Not one to give up easily, I decided we could figure it out. The sales potential was too hard to pass up: they had already become our top-selling nut at farmers market, and stores and coffee shops had expressed interest. Surely the recipe couldn't be *that* hard to figure out.

To replace some of the agave, we tried Sucanat, a dry, granulated sugar that wouldn't add stickiness to the nuts. Sucanat—which stands for Sugar Cane Natural—was the least-processed cane sugar available. Jared and I tried one ratio after another. Invariably, improving one aspect hurt another. With more Sucanat, the nuts weren't as glossy or shiny, reducing their eye appeal. With more agave, they were too sticky; with more cinnamon, too dark. And on and on with all the possibilities we tried—for months. Because the Cinnamon Almonds were so popular, and almonds our least-costly nut, I had great incentive. But after at least a dozen attempts, varying the recipe each time, we let them go—we could never solve the stickiness factor. Because of the labor involved, they were simply not a good use of Jared's time.

In the end, my foray into flavored, roasted nuts did not yield the sales results I wanted. Although I was proud of myself for creating a unique product line, my creations were different enough to be problematic, especially concerning shelf placement. They were expensive and unfamiliar. Since flavored nuts were not an established market category, stores were hesitant to add them. A few local stores and coffee shops ordered in our small bags, and Whole Foods tried them in bulk for a while.

Although Chipotle Pecans were among those I abandoned, I wasn't willing to give up on a chipotle-flavored nut. I switched the pecans to peanuts—not only were they delicious, but they cost one-third as much. Chipotle Peanuts soon became our best seller both online and at farmers market.

The tagline for the nuts came to me on a walk with Jouey: "I'm Perfectly Nutty!" "Perfectly" fit in with some of my other taglines, and I certainly felt "nutty" to have put so much effort into them. I thought my nut creations would have a bright future, but continual price increases and persistent marketing challenges caused them to meet with limited success. The Google office in Boulder bought the Chipotle Peanuts as a snack for its employees, local gift basket companies purchased them, and we continued to sell them online and at farmers market—but production was more a labor of love than a contributing factor to our bottom line.

*   *   *

Sales were on the rise, making another box run necessary. With the bank account in the black, I could afford it. New boxes allowed us to drop the Kosher certification. We didn't have distribution on the east coast to justify it, and the rabbis, as friendly as they were, tended to pop in at the worst possible times for their random inspections. Some days, the interruptions prevented us from completing our scheduled production run.

I also modified one of the granola varieties: Cinnamon Raisin turned into Cinnamon Spice. The former had never gained much of a following, and customers continued to give me negative feedback about raisins. I didn't want to discontinue the variety since it would leave Orange Crunch as the only option for customers who were allergic to nuts. To "spice" it up, I added nutmeg; it offered a subtle flavor that was a bit mysterious, and the result was delicious. We also added my signature to the boxes, underneath my drawing, to accommodate requests over the years for my autograph.

We were receiving more publicity—articles in local newspapers and television coverage of the company and me—all of which helped bring wider distribution, new accounts, and stellar sales in the first six months of 2008, including new regions of the country. I buzzed around like a little bee, doing my best to keep up with it all. My granola world was happy once again.

As exciting as anything else, I was able to make extra payments toward the bank loan, in large chunks. Paying off that loan was my No. 1 goal. Further, I had made a commitment to myself there would be *no more loans*. I would expand as much as possible without borrowing more money; if that meant keeping the company small, so be it.

I was equally excited about the pending move into Leonard's facility. He had found a building in Longmont that had been damaged by fire but was structurally sound and suitable to use as a food manufacturing plant. It would not be off the grid, as original plans had called for, but could be converted to solar if technology came to justify the cost and time.

I ended my lease with Steve by allowing other tenants to fill my space. He wished me well and said he would continue to be a customer. He and his wife eventually opened a coffee shop in the business park, and they ordered my granola as a menu item.

We were completely moved in by the end of July. Since sales had been strong the first half of the year, there was no reason to think that would change. Like millions of other people, we had no idea what was brewing on the financial horizon—with the bank and real estate investment schemes taking place behind closed doors.

Suddenly, like a sharp slap in the face, sales plummeted. UNFI orders dropped by 50 percent, and Sysco by 20 percent. Many local accounts, mostly cafes and coffee shops, dropped my line completely. They needed to tighten their purse strings, they said, and were switching to less-expensive mainstream brands. Some of the restaurants began baking their own granola. Sales waned both online and at farmers market. In response, we streamlined our production and became more efficient. Although revenue dropped significantly, my company managed to stay profitable.

Though my relationship with Leonard began on a positive note, it was soon tested. He was upset that as soon as my company moved into his facility, sales nosedived. Leonard felt it was because my sales and marketing efforts had become lax, and didn't believe that nothing had changed on my part. He lost confidence my company would grow enough to pay the higher rent he was hoping to charge so he could finance his expansion plans. Because of this, he said, I would need to share my space and equipment with other food manufacturers. Although the idea did not appeal to me, I saw his point: If my sales couldn't cover the increased rent he wanted, revenue from other companies could fill the gap.

Finding these companies and arranging for them to move in took time, though. For the first year or so, mine was the only one using the facility. Slowly and steadily, more tenants arrived. Space was consolidated and production schedules created. Operations proceeded reasonably well, but over time, we tenants felt the strain of sharing close quarters. Ingredient mishaps, equipment misunderstandings, scheduling and cleaning conflicts, storage disagreements, and space configuration issues became common. Some days, we went on treasure hunts to find our utensils and supplies. Other days, there were production delays and interruptions. The environment became a bit chaotic. As our areas became increasingly dense, we renters became a tight-knit community. Tenants and their employees pitched in for the common good. Workers cross-trained and put in hours with other companies, which helped everyone. We learned from each other and genuinely wished each other well. Sometimes we shared our brokers and suppliers, at other times our knowledge and expertise.

The workplace situation was difficult sometimes, but the swirl of activity also generated friendly interaction and goodwill. The energy in the bakery was positive and optimistic, upbeat music filled the air, and our senses of humor tempered frustrations. We all understood that we were in a challenging situation, and we supported each other through our meandering maze of activity in our tight quarters.

Product challenges were numerous. Because so many food items were being produced simultaneously, conflicting aromas, humidity levels, and temperature fluctuations affected all our products. We learned to be flexible and open-minded, and our communal involvement gave us compassion for each other's situation. We were a motley crew and did the best we could to keep ourselves afloat and help each other along the way.

Operational challenges rose from the fact that although the other tenants understood that I owned the equipment and office furniture, their contracts with Leonard gave them the right to use it. Ongoing maintenance and forgotten repairs created stress for us all.

Leonard had plenty of challenges too. The varied production requirements were dizzying, yet he set up a schedule that allowed each of us to manufacture and package our products. His wife was an engineer and helped with facility operations. Both had worked in manufacturing, and they understood equipment well. Leonard could fix just about anything and did repairs with ease and grace.

One day, though, the situation took an unexpected toll on my operation. Jared called to ask if he could stop by my house. I could tell by his tone of voice that the conversation would not be a happy one. The chaotic environment had become too much, he said. He missed the solitary surroundings we'd had before, and the quiet that came with it. His resignation brought tears to my eyes. He had become the most talented and trustworthy baker I'd ever had the pleasure to work with. His calm presence and simple lifestyle were beautiful to see. I admired him like a son.

Eventually, Leonard and I reached a financial resolution: He would buy the equipment and relinquish all equity in the company. I repaid the $25,000 he and his wife had loaned me for the earlier box production run.

~18~

THE DECISION TO SELL

"The purpose of life is a life of purpose."
—Robert Byrne
(Quote on a box of Toasted Almond Granola)

D uring this time, I fell in love. I had met Jon on the bus from Boulder to the Denver airport as Natalie and I were on our way to Italy for my parents' fiftieth wedding anniversary celebration. Jon and his daughter were going to the airport to meet his mother.

As usual, I was late getting the two of us to where we needed to be—this time, the park-and-ride. I was afraid we'd miss our bus to the airport, which meant we'd miss our flight to Italy. We whipped into the parking structure and had to climb three levels before finding a spot. "Run, honey!" I said. "Run as fast as you can to meet the bus! We absolutely *have* to catch that ride to the airport!"

Natalie was eleven at the time. Those little legs took off running down the stairwell, suitcase in tow, while I unloaded the rest of our belongings and followed. When I got to street level, I quickly glanced around. What I saw allowed me to breathe: people waiting, with their suitcases, for the bus to arrive. I found Natalie and hollered, "Woo, hoo! Give me five, honey! We're gonna catch our flight after all!" We gave each other a high five, even though my enthusiasm embarrassed her. Other passengers looked at us, somewhat amused. I asked Natalie to get in line so she could find two seats together while I got our luggage on the bus.

When I found her near the back, I sat down with a huge sigh and gave her a big hug. "Thank you, honey," I said. "Sorry this was such a hectic adventure. But we made it, and we can relax now." Then I glanced to my right. Sitting there, on the other side of the aisle, was

Jon, next to his daughter, who was a few years younger than Natalie. We started chatting, and the girls joined in occasionally. We struck a nice rapport, and a noticeable spark flew between us. By the time we got to the airport, we had learned a little about each other. He lived in the mountains but worked in Boulder at the National Center for Atmospheric Research, designing scientific software. He had bought my granola in the past, and said he'd stop by farmers market.

Long story short, he visited the market, we started dating, and married about a year later. I sold my condo, he sold his house, and we bought a home in Boulder. He, like me, shared custody of his daughter, and the girls got along well. Marrying Jon and starting new lives together let me feel more stable than I had in a long time.

In addition to being a wonderful companion, he became an immediate asset to my company. Using his software design skills, he created small labels that mimicked the look of my boxes; I used them to make packets for demos and sales calls. He joined me occasionally at market and kept tabs on the cereals and energy bars when out shopping. He even got my products into the employee cafeteria where he worked and at another scientific facility. Jon had innovative marketing ideas and seemed to enjoy helping with the business. I was grateful to have him by my side.

I found two new bakers who were cheerful and friendly and seemed to enjoy their work. Jared was next door with another food company, so we saw each other occasionally. I made a habit of dropping by the bakery more often, which let me establish a closer relationship with my employees and the other renters. There was a constant buzz in the bakery, with lots of camaraderie. Things were chaotic, to be sure, and the frustrations and problems of sharing space with numerous renters never went away. Still, we helped each other as much as possible. Perhaps best of all, because of Leonard's equipment purchase, I was able to pay off the bank loan five years early. With that burden out of my life, I could relax even more. Although the recession was in full swing, major accounts were expanding enough that my sales still climbed, and the business's bank account steadily grew.

*   *   *

Before I knew it, another market season was upon me, and customers were asking, as they did at the start of each year, "So what new product do you have for us?" They must have thought I had nothing better to do during the off months than dream up new foods. Yet my audience was eager, and I wasn't about to turn down potential new revenue. Developing a new product each season was a win-win for everyone. Customers enjoyed trying new goodies, and I unleashed my creativity. It kept the business fresh for me.

I enjoyed all aspects of product development: creating something new and giving it a good name, running the nutritionals, figuring out the pricing, creating a tagline, deciding how best to market it, choosing colors, and creating the artwork and labels. The birth of each product was similar to that of a child. A new personality, distinct attributes, unique qualities, and different challenges, discoveries, and delights. Each was a new source of pride.

Despite the sales flop the nuts had been, I created another snack food but opted for something simple: Trail Mix. We already had dried fruit, nuts, and seeds in inventory, so the formulation was easy. On a hike one day, while eating one of the mixes, the names came to me: Jungle Blend and Mountain Blend. Jungle Blend had walnuts, almonds, cranberries, pepitas, and papaya. Mountain Blend had almonds, Brazil nuts, cranberries, raisins, pepitas, and dark chocolate chips. On hot days, I only brought Jungle Blend to farmers market. The chocolate chips in the Mountain Blend melted in the heat and smeared the inside of the bags.

I was pleased with my creations and put on my sales cap. Although they were more expensive than other trail mixes, they were well received in coffee shops, local stores, at farmers market, and via our website. Gift basket companies ordered four-ounce and ten-ounce bags, and Whole Foods brought both varieties into bulk. They sold well everywhere, including in a Longmont market that specialized in gourmet bulk items.

My life felt calmer than it had in years. Sales were up, and the creative aspects of running the company dominated day-to-day operations. Natalie continued to enjoy farmers market, and the two of us had fun managing our booth. She had taken up tennis, and we enjoyed playing together; I'd been an avid tennis player earlier in life, and our abilities were well matched. The girls got along, and Jon and I were very much in love. Life seemed good, and I did my best to put the stress of earlier years behind me. I focused on my health and tried to gain back the weight I had lost. Jon and I traveled. We had committed to an out-of-the-country trip each year; our first was to Guatemala. For the first time in a long time, I participated in activities that had nothing to do with running a business; I felt grateful to restore at least a little balance to my life.

Natalie was in middle school, located in our neighborhood, and I worked from home. During those years, she allowed me to spend one full day at school with her each year—this was to help me get over my sorrow that I had never done that in elementary school. Some days, I biked to meet her after school so we could bike home together. Later on, during her high school years, when her school was on the other end of town, I often walked to the bus stop to meet her so we could walk home together.

During that time, I found the energy and creativity to start my e-newsletter. I had planned this since the company's inception, and had even written one early on; it was posted on my website. Yet with all the craziness, I'd never had time to launch it—despite many requests over the years.

Once I started, I found the newsletters to be a wonderful outlet for self-expression and creative writing. My goals were to educate customers and increase sales by generating interest in the product line. Starting in September 2010, I rarely missed a month. I enjoyed coming up with health topics, seasonally related items, and other tidbits. I had an assistant to coordinate the social media marketing. We included recipe and photo contests and encouraged readers to like us on Facebook and follow us on Twitter. We also sent short announcement-type newsletters to introduce the nuts and trail mixes, and to publicize updates, such as when Cinnamon Raisin granola became Cinnamon Spice, or Almond Blueberry Peach Quinoa Crunch reentered the market after a brief hiatus. Recipes included quinoa-crusted catfish, banana orange walnut bread, peach cobbler, brownies with nut topping, chocolate chip cookies, raspberry granola squares, quinoa hazelnut salad, and chile rellenos, all made with products from my line.

I suspect there was very little correlation between increased sales and the amount of time and effort I put into those newsletters. But our contact list grew steadily, and I received much positive feedback. Just as important, I enjoyed writing them and connecting with customers in a new way.

*　*　*

My ability to enjoy the activity and social aspects of Leonard's production facility was short-lived. Boulder had become a hub for the natural products industry, and food production space was in high demand. Leonard enlarged the facility and continually brought in more renters. It was a good business move on his part, but the quality of my products suffered. Because the ovens were used around the clock, the bakery rarely cooled down completely, which meant our products took longer to cool. Wheat had been introduced into the facility, which made our "wheat free" claim questionable. Sundry aromas filled the air, and I worried that our products would absorb the flavors of other foods. Equipment needed repair more often because of its high use. The ongoing build-out generated a good deal of dust and debris. The bakery swarmed with activity and people, from food manufacturers to construction workers. I no longer enjoyed the ambience, and kept my visits as short and infrequent as possible.

My stress level started to climb—and my marriage started to suffer. Disharmony threatened to replace the bliss. Jon and I began having parenting disagreements, and they did not have easy solutions. Even a romantic getaway to Ecuador didn't bring our relationship back to where it had been. The girls became withdrawn, from both each other and from us. That was perhaps hardest of all. Natalie and I had always been close, and I felt her backing away. I couldn't blame her—she could sense the stress and felt the need to distance herself. Still, I was not okay with it. I blamed the changing dynamics of the marriage. Jon blamed the stress of the business. He claimed I had become more irritable and short-tempered, an observation I could not deny.

In addition to my other challenges, Boulder was home to a growing number of granola companies. For quite a few years, I had been the only cereal manufacturer. But competition had moved in, and I was feeling the pinch. Some new companies were aggressive and tried to lure accounts away with offers of free fill and lower prices. Most were allowed into farmers market. There also were more cereal companies on the national scene. New granolas on the shelf at Whole Foods took a toll on my bottom line. Furthermore, my costs for ingredients, labor, rent, packaging, and distribution were on the rise.

Another reason I felt the pinch of lost sales had nothing to do with competition. Instead, it had to do with gluten. Many of my customers had gone gluten free, but my granola contained gluten because of the barley. My efforts to create a line of gluten-free granolas did not leave me feeling proud. Without the barley, the granola just wasn't the same. It lost its complexity and heartiness, the flavor was not as robust, and the texture was inferior. I tried grain after grain but couldn't find a viable substitute. I'd been lucky with product development up until then. Not only was this a blow to my ego, it was a blow to my pocketbook due to lost sales because of the gluten. Depression and worry set in, both in my personal and professional life.

The stress exhausted me on every level. I felt that all I could offer had been squeezed out of me. I was ready for time off—for true rest and relaxation—and I knew the only way to achieve it would be to separate myself from the business. I would no longer let my company be more important than my personal life. I thought that with less stress, my relationship with Natalie would go back to the way it had been. Perhaps Jon and I would reignite the spark that had faded. Maybe our marriage would recover. He had been patient and generous with his time. I could tell he didn't enjoy helping with the company as much as he had initially, and I couldn't blame him. I thought that by selling the company, uncertainties would fade away, and my health and relationships would be restored.

I reminded myself of a promise I had made early on: "When I quit having fun, I'll quit." After ten years, that time had arrived. I still felt dedicated to the company's success, but didn't have the strength to keep it going. One last investment opportunity came my way—one that was fair and with people I respected and enjoyed. That one tugged at me, but I let it go. I knew in my heart it was time to sell.

The day I had called my parents, a decade earlier, to tell them I planned to start a granola company, there was palpable nervousness and disapproval on the other end of the phone. The day I called to say I planned to sell the company, there was a similar stunned silence. It didn't last long. My mother was the first to reply. "Thank goodness!" she exclaimed. "That's the best news we've heard in a while. You don't need that stress in your life any longer." My father's response, not surprisingly, was less emotional. "Thanks for letting us know," he said.

I called the chamber and learned that a "How to Sell Your Business" workshop would be presented the following week. The facilitator, Suzanne, was knowledgeable and approachable. We discussed my business, and she agreed to take me on as a client.

Suzanne was fun and easy to work with. She educated me on the intricacies of selling a business, and had me gather financials and other details about the company's structure, organization, history, and general health. Some of the process was tedious, other parts were fun, and through it all, I learned a lot about the value and marketability of my company.

~19~
CHALLENGING TRANSITIONS

*"If we clear a space, it is often filled with
the answers we need."*

—Anonymous

For the better part of 2011, I had tried unsuccessfully to create gluten-free granolas. We were losing too much market share by not offering them. I also knew that any buyer of the company would expect to have them as part of the product line. I dug in my heels again. My goal was twofold: find a good substitute for barley, and create unique flavor combinations. I had one more product line to produce, and this would be it.

I had already tried ground sorghum, millet, rice, and quinoa as barley substitutes. None had adhered to the oats or complemented the texture.

One day, my eyes fell on the ground flax seeds in the bakery's warehouse. "Hmmm," I thought. "I wonder how these would pair with the oats?" The next morning, I mixed up a test batch. After it cooled, I tasted it. "Wow!" I thought. "This is pretty good!" The flavor and texture were better than the results from my earlier attempts, and time was running short. I had much to do to get the business ready to sell, and my patience for creating this new product line had already worn thin.

With flax seeds as my new hero, I began to experiment with different flavor combinations. Customers had always asked for a variety with vanilla. I'd experimented with this early on but could barely taste it in the finished product, and decided it wasn't worth the extra cost. But since this new line needed new flavors, I decided vanilla would be one of them. Because gluten-free oats and flax seeds didn't absorb the vanilla like regular oats and barley had, the flavor was noticeable. In short order, the first variety was ready: Vanilla Coconut. The coconut and vanilla both stood out. Everyone who tried it loved it. *Whew*.

On to the next flavor. With nut allergies on the rise, I decided it would be wise to create a second flavor without nuts. After a bit of experimenting, I came up with Cranberry Flax. All the gluten-free varieties contained flax, but I liked the name and only had to add cranberries to the base recipe to create a new flavor. It was also well received.

Only one to go! The granola varieties with almonds had always been our top sellers, so I added them to the last variety. Adding the almonds didn't give the flair I expected—I was after more crunch. One day, I found whole millet seeds in my pantry and thought, "What the heck?" I threw some in the mix. The Almond Millet became my instant favorite of the three varieties.

Happy at last with my new creations, I turned my focus to the packaging. I ordered clear standup pouch bags, and Jon created labels by incorporating the main features of the box design. We added the cereals to the website, brought them to farmers market, and easily got them into the stores. Most of the buyers said, "It's about time, Fiona! What took you so long?"

*   *   *

Suzanne and I had our ducks in a row by the end of September. By mid-November, a few parties had expressed interest. One family in particular was keen to learn about day-to-day operations, sales forecasts, and cash flow. They visited the bakery, then asked for a second visit to see a typical production day. We obliged. After that, they requested more detailed financials, which we supplied.

A couple of weeks later, Suzanne called. "You sitting down?" she asked. I wasn't but I found a chair.

"Yes," I replied.

"Good, because I have some exciting news," she said. The family had made an offer. It was based on a common valuation formula of sales multiples. Although it wasn't the millions of dollars most people had suggested I would get, I was good with it. The offer included keeping me on as an integral part of the business, for the life of the company, if I chose. I was offered a respectable salary, with my own office—which I could paint any color under the sun. I was flattered, but I was also burned out. I agreed to work until the end of the year, then decide whether to stay longer.

The sale was finalized on February 15, 2012. Suzanne said it was record time to list a business and ink a deal. I couldn't help but feel good that I had started and grown a company that would attract a buyer so quickly. After details of the sale were complete, and a turquoise-and-lime-green office was ready for me, we got to work.

The first six months, I basically taught the new owner, Jarrett, everything I could about running the business. He learned quickly and had some new ideas for marketing and product development. Because his family had a vested interest in the sunflower seed business, he wished to feature the seeds in a few products. We added sunflower seeds to the Coconut Vanilla gluten-free granola and changed the name to Sunflower Vanilla Coconut. We also replaced the expensive nuts in both varieties of Trail Mix with sunflower seeds and peanuts, which reduced the overall cost.

The months passed, and we transitioned into our different roles. Our offices were just a mile from Leonard's facility, which made it easy to go back and forth. I relished working in a new environment. The commute was easy, and I enjoyed social interactions at both locations. Dynamics had changed with the purchase, which allowed my communications at the bakery to be more social and less business-like.

Jarrett's goal was to take the products national as quickly as possible. He chose not to put much effort on the smaller accounts, and to have all accounts order from our distributors. I'd never minded handling small orders from the businesses that didn't use our distributors, such as gift basket companies, coffee shops, and specialty stores. They kept me face-to-face with the buyers, all of whom had helped my products gain traction over the years. But Jarrett decided that to focus our efforts on growth and expansion, those small accounts needed to go.

He also felt we shouldn't participate in farmers market, and that my time could be better spent. Natalie and I still loved doing market, and wanted to stay. We compromised by hiring someone to be there every other week. That way, Natalie and I could run the booth together, and Jon and I would have alternate weekends to ourselves, since our daughters were on the same weekend parenting schedule. In theory, this could have worked well. It didn't. I missed doing market, and Jon and I didn't go away for weekends as we had thought we would. Much of my social life over the previous ten years had been at market, and when that changed, I felt the void. Eventually, I worked the booth most Saturdays. I enjoyed keeping the connection with my customers, the other vendors, and friends and acquaintances who were regulars. When I did want a Saturday off, we hired someone to run the booth.

One sunny morning, Jarrett and I were in our offices when a call came. It was the police. Dennis, our baker, had been reported for violating parole and was waiting in handcuffs to be taken away. When I'd hired him the previous year, he said he had learned to bake in prison. Dennis was passionate about baking and promised to do a great job. He seemed like a good kid and was honest about his past. The last thing he wanted, he said, was to return to jail. I'm a firm believer in giving people a second chance and believed he wouldn't do anything to put himself back there.

We rushed to the bakery and found him outside with the officers; they couldn't say how long his sentence would be. He was our only baker, and we were barely keeping up with orders. Jarrett and I exchanged glances, taking in the situation. We needed a replacement, fast. As luck would have it, there were two young men working part-time for other companies at the bakery. They had already helped bake granola on occasion after I had trained them during a different crisis the previous year. Both were sociable, friendly, fast learners, and fun to work with; they agreed to fit us in part-time. To complement their hours, though, Jarrett and I would have to jump in. He had wanted to learn the baking process anyway, so this would be the perfect opportunity.

The next few months were rough. I had many a ten-hour day at the bakery, most of them on my feet. Until our new full-time baker and part-time packager were fully trained, I pretty much moved my office into the bakery to supervise production and help with the baking and packaging. Our inventory was low, sales were on the rise, and we were gaining new accounts; keeping inventory stocked was paramount. Eventually, everyone was fully trained, and we felt a huge relief not to be dependent on just one baker; all of us except the packager could bake cereals or bars, blend trail mix or muesli, and roast the nuts. Through Jarrett's family connections, we hired a University of Colorado aeronautical engineering major to help package once a week. The equipment was complex, but he learned his way around the machines instantly and was a joy to have around.

Dennis's replacement as our baker was someone we knew we were taking a chance on. Ian had been a meth addict, and we were hesitant. What if his habit resurfaced? What if the drugs had left him debilitated? Could we rely on him? But of all the candidates, he had the most baking experience. He seemed upfront, honest, and sincere. Not only had he been clean for over two years, but he also had full-time custody of his eight-year-old daughter. If he stepped out of line, he would lose that. I told Jarrett we should take a chance on him, and in the end, he agreed. Although Ian learned more slowly than some of his predecessors, he became a skilled baker and one of our most reliable employees. He managed to juggle full-time fatherhood with a full-time job, and he thrived in both. With Ian fully trained, I moved back to my office.

The Maya belief that 2012 would signal great change, that one cycle would end and another would begin, certainly held true for me. Because I was accustomed to running the business a certain way, I felt at odds with some of Jarrett's changes. They were in the name of efficiency and higher profits, so I understood his reasoning. As I'd expected, we lost some of my favorite accounts, small businesses that had been among the first to take a chance on my products. Without their initial support, Fiona's would not have gained the traction it did. I felt a loyalty to them that the new owners understandably did not.

In addition, I was being asked to justify my view on certain aspects of the business that I felt sure about. It seemed my competence was being questioned. That did not sit well.

I no longer felt I had the flexibility for my daily walks, hikes, and bike rides, and I wasn't home when Natalie got there as I used to be. Although she enjoyed having the house to herself, I missed seeing her right after school and was convinced she didn't share as much about her day, since by the time we saw each other, the events were not as fresh in her mind.

The year was coming to an end, and I had a decision to make: continue or resign? I consulted with Jon. He could see how run down I was. I felt drained, physically and emotionally; I was ready to slow down and recover from the demands of the past eleven years. Natalie was a sophomore in high school, so our time together was winding down. Friends and school activities kept her busy, which meant less time for the two of us; I loved the thought of gaining a little of it back. I had paid off our house in Boulder with the proceeds of the sale, so living expenses were minimal. Jon had a stable job, so between that and the fact that there was no mortgage, we didn't need two incomes. He said he would support me in whatever I chose to do. I took a deep breath and let out a long sigh. "Okay," I told him, "in that case, I'll resign. I think it'll do us a lot of good."

When I told Jarrett, he didn't seem surprised. He could see how ragged I had become, and he thought the decision to take time off was a good one. He told me he and his family had hoped I would stay for the life of the company, that they truly enjoyed working with me, and that they would miss me. We left the door open to the possibility I would return someday—although I think we both knew that would probably never happen. I put in two more weeks, packed up my belongings, and left. That was mid-December, 2012.

~20~
NEW INSPIRATIONS

"Life can only be understood backwards, but it must be lived forwards."

—Søren Kierkegaard
(Quote on boxes of Cherry Pecan Muesli)

The following year, I decompressed. In February, Jon and I spent a week in Puerto Vallarta to celebrate the sale of the business. I took classes, just for fun: photography, first aid, and three writing classes. I put on my chef's hat and cooked creative meals for the family. I added to my blogsite. In October, I went to Oaxaca for three weeks to brush up on my Spanish. In addition, I wholeheartedly began to declutter my life. The basement looked like a tsunami had passed through. It had flooded twice, and I'd never taken the time to properly sort through what was left. For the better part of the year, I focused on ridding my life of belongings. Every donated carload lightened my spirit not only physically but also emotionally. With fewer belongings in the basement, clothes in the closets, books on the shelves, and items in drawers, I felt an increased sense of lightness and well-being.

I could not bear, however, to part with anything Natalie had created over the years. I kept all her schoolwork and artwork. I kept photos and writings, family memorabilia, and letters stuffed away in long-forgotten boxes. I kept business files, Spanish teaching materials, art, music, and genealogy records. Almost everything else I set free: books that would never be read, clothes that would never be worn, utensils that would never be used, toys, puzzles, art, jewelry . . . and so much more.

The following year, Jon and I went to Ireland. Our relationship had improved, mostly because of less stress on my part. I enjoyed being home when Natalie returned from school. I went to her tennis tournaments and other school activities, and the two of us played tennis together regularly. I caught up on eleven years of sleep deprivation, and I found a naturopath who delved into my health issues. Natalie and I went to England to visit my sister and her family. They had been there eight years, but this was our first visit.

Later that year, I was invited to present a talk as part of a women's entrepreneur series. I would have to write a speech encompassing the highs and lows of owning my granola company. I hesitated, mostly because I was in de-stress mode and didn't want the stress of the past to resurface. Eventually I agreed; to my surprise, I enjoyed sharing both the joys and the difficulties of my story. Writing the speech reminded me that many people over the years had encouraged me to write a book about my granola journey. The speech gave me a hint of what that would involve. After the talk, I received wonderful feedback and more encouragement to write a book. I added it to my list of considerations.

During 2013 and 2014, with Jon at work and Natalie in school, I spent a lot of time alone. It was a definitive step toward imagining what my future might hold. My reflections led to realizations that were surprising and enlightening. It was as if I were viewing myself as an outsider, from a perspective I hadn't seen before. The time alone was a springboard that would catapult me to the next phase of my journey.

During this time, Natalie and I went to a Dale Chihuly sculpture exhibit at the Denver Botanic Gardens, and watched a video there in which he described how his unique form and style of art had developed. Spending a great deal of time alone during a Fulbright year in Venice had been pivotal for his creativity. Thoughts and ideas gelled at a time when he was young, impressionable, and open to artistic inspiration. Even to this day, he said, he spends two to three hours alone in the early morning, contemplating art and forms that are yet to be created.

Although many people don't enjoy being alone, for the artistically inclined, solitude can help to spawn creativity. Whether the result is to write a song, color a canvas, design a food product, throw clay, carve a sculpture, sew a quilt, build an instrument, or start a nonprofit . . . whatever the creative act may be, time alone lets the imagination and vision unfold. I found peace with my solitude and recognized the value it offered.

*　*　*

After selling the company, I was free to be creative on other paths. During those contemplative months in which I lightened my load, decompressed, and focused on my health and family, a new spark ignited. It wanted to be fed. I sat with this new energy and contemplated how best to nurture it. I found my copy of *The Artist's Way* by Julia Cameron. Jon had given me the book and accompanying *Morning Pages* journal after I sold the company. The book was a revelation—I savored each chapter, and I dutifully wrote three pages each morning. My writing pulled more from the depths of my soul than I could have imagined. I completed half the tasks set forth in each chapter, as suggested. I took myself on Artist Dates. The activities brought an abundance of epiphanies into my world. Cameron validated what I had held sacred: the importance of leading a creative life—and the importance of *allowing* ourselves such a life. Her emphasis that creativity is not only paramount to our existence, but necessary for our happiness, brought a huge sense of satisfaction. It also explained—in poignant prose—why I had managed my company the way I had. New inspiration bubbled forth. What called out most strongly was to follow the many suggestions and words of encouragement to tell my story. Thus, the writing of this book began.

Although my relationship with Jon had improved after the sale of the business, our marriage didn't make it. We had survived a lot of stress, but it had taken its toll. Our parenting styles were different, the girls never bonded as we hoped they would, and the four of us never bonded as a family. We each made compromises, but those concessions pulled on the very fabric that held us together. The threads had worn thin. Instead of continued compromises, which would tug at our fragile ties even more, we decided it was best to part. Our relationship had been harmonious, the two of us had been the best of friends, and we still loved each other. But we knew that staying together was not in the best interests of our daughters or our own relationships with them. I will always feel indebted to Jon—his endless generosity and patience during those very stressful times helped me weather the turbulent storms.

One day, long after I had sold the company, I went to a downtown street fair; I was sampling something when a woman asked if I was Fiona. She had recognized me from the drawing on the back of the cereal boxes. She said she loved the Orange Crunch and that it was the only granola her daughter would eat. I froze, because Jarrett had told me he would be discontinuing that variety. I didn't have the heart to tell her. I didn't want to spoil the moment because her daughter was there, and they seemed thrilled at the chance to tell me how much they loved the cereal. Later, I regretted not telling her, because she could have stocked up before the stores stopped carrying it. That occasion reminded me why I hadn't passed off the reins any earlier. For the new owners, it was a simple business decision: The varieties that brought in lower revenues would have to go. Although Orange Crunch wasn't a top seller, it certainly had a devoted following.

Soon afterward, I received a phone call from an independent grocery in California. The owner said he'd called my cell because no one had picked up at the office. He had called specifically to order Orange Crunch, and I had to inform him the new owners had discontinued it. There was silence at the other end of the phone. "Oh," he replied slowly as the information sank in. "Well, I'm sure gonna have a lot of disappointed customers." I told him I was also disappointed but that it was a decision I no longer controlled. Sometimes, customers stopped me in the street to ask what had happened to Orange Crunch, and Natalie's high school tennis coach said she stopped eating granola when she could no longer find it. Knowing that fans would be disappointed was hard for me, especially since my name on the package implied I had something to do with the decision.

Through the years, my own granola consumption rotated among Ginger Walnut, Toasted Almond, and Orange Crunch. I was in Orange Crunch mode when I learned it would be discontinued. Although I knew how to make it, that wasn't the same as having it available in the stores; I would also miss seeing that pretty orange box on supermarket shelves.

As owner of my company, I had placed importance on listening to customers and doing my best to offer what they requested. Even if I only broke even on those products, they had their purpose. My business wasn't only about the bottom line—it was also about making people smile, keeping customers happy, and providing products that couldn't be found elsewhere. Through the years, that's how some of my most popular products were created.

I had altered the original Ginger Walnut recipe early on for a friend whose irritable bowel syndrome kept her from tolerating sesame seeds, which were in all the granolas at the time. Just for her, I removed them from one variety. I created Cinnamon Almond for my friend Joy who loved the Toasted Almond but couldn't tolerate coconut. What a "joy" that turned out to be—the Cinnamon Almond was our number two seller for all the years I owned the company. I created the muesli for the French chef who wanted to add a European flair to his menu. The granola bars also resulted from customer requests, and I created the gluten-free products for buyers who had eliminated gluten from their diets.

*   *   *

While I'd been busy clearing my clutter and writing this book, more inspiration came in. I thought of a new product line to create, one I believed could meet with great success. "I must be totally insane," I thought. "Start a new company, after all I've been through?" Still, a new food company would feed my creative side and allow growth in new directions. The lessons learned the first time would be my building blocks for this next endeavor. The power of creation is irresistible, as is the joy of following one's heart and pursuing one's passions.

Natalie was in high school when I began the product development for a second food company. She critiqued the goodies and had ideas for new varieties, presentations, flavors, and ingredients. Since childhood, she had exhibited a distinctly keen palate. Whether it was genetic or came from growing up with a mom who created new food products and wanted her feedback will remain a mystery. Over the years, for each new product, I'd solicited her opinion: Is it sweet enough? Does it need salt? How's the texture? The consistency? Would your friends like it? Her ability to discern flavors was astounding, and her suggested improvements were spot on.

The idea for my new company would be to create custom products that let customers choose the flavors, ingredient combinations, sizes, and shapes. That kind of business model is rare but it truly honors the customers—the very people who purchase our products and whose appreciation helps us thrive. I'm not sure I'll pursue the second company, but if I do, the recipes are ready to go, and with them, a built-in mechanism for variations that can easily be modified to meet customer requests.

~21~
DEFINING SUCCESS

"Be the change you wish to see in the world."
—Mohandas Gandhi
(Quote on boxes of Orange Crunch Granola)

W hile immersed in *The Artist's Way*, I continued my outdoor adventures. I took many wonderful hikes in which I contemplated what I would do next with my life. I could process my thoughts and let silence enter. Those hikes, quiet and uninterrupted, became walking meditations.

My projects continued. I compiled photo albums for Natalie's graduation present and wrote posts for my blog. I put time into my new food company and completed a travel career course. I volunteered for nonprofit organizations and attended Spanish conversation groups. Natalie and I played tennis, and we visited farmers market. The introspection continued.

One night, I watched a total lunar eclipse. As the moon disappeared and then reappeared, I analyzed the previous twelve years of my life. I recalled a hike I'd been on one day—I'd stopped to chat with a friend who also owned a small food company. She asked how things were going. I told her that growth was slow but steady. She replied, "You know, Fiona, of all the food companies in Boulder, yours has the greatest opportunity for major success and expansion. I'm surprised you haven't gone national yet, and so are others. You need to figure out what's holding you back! And what you're afraid of." With that, she continued up the mountain.

I pondered what she'd said, but not for long. Years passed, and although I'd forgotten about our interaction, the conversation came back to me during that eclipse. Had I been afraid of something all those years? Had something been holding me back? Suddenly, the answer was clear: Yes, I had been afraid of something, and indeed, something had held me back. I wasn't afraid of success; I deserved that as much as anybody. Instead, I was afraid of a work regimen that would take away the ability to control my hours and make my own schedule. I was also afraid that my creativity would be taken away. I was holding myself back, and for reasons some people might never understand. With that question finally answered, a sense of peace came over me. The decision to keep my company small was my answer to holding on to the flexibility and creativity I so cherished. I almost jumped out of my deck chair in the middle of the night to call her. We hadn't spoken in years, but I thought she might finally like an answer to her question.

My focus—maintaining a flexible schedule with Natalie and creativity for myself—had dictated much of the destiny of my company. Without the *joie de vivre* that inextricably comes when we feed our creative sides, we can be left with a feeling of emptiness. In running the company, the more I nourished my creativity, the more empowered I felt. What jazzed me each day was the ability to develop new products, figure out the packaging, explore new venues for my creations, and personally introduce them to my customers.

How do we define success, and how do we define happiness? Many people do it monetarily. If we are successful, we must have a lot of money. If we are happy, we must be financially sound. In the spring of 2014, a woman from Paraguay came to one of my Spanish meetup groups. She was delightful: bubbly, fun, and spirited. In Paraguay, most people live at the poverty level. Yet a Gallup poll had rated the country as the "happiest" in the world.

When the man sitting next to me heard this, he replied, "So I guess that means money isn't what makes people happy." That led to an interesting discussion about what makes a person truly happy. A TED Talk later that year demonstrated that happiness comes about when we live a life consistent with our values. If there is congruency with our values and the life we lead, we will find happiness. And because all our values differ, the route to happiness has many paths.

As my company had expanded, I'd become more apathetic about how my products did the farther from home they went. Knowing my granola was sitting on supermarket shelves in Texas didn't make me feel any happier. Instead, it made me nervous that I needed to support those stores with demos, promos, and marketing. I couldn't check on the stores personally or get to know the employees. Those stores seemed fictional to me in a sense, simply because I had never seen them or met anyone who worked there. I felt loyalty to, and support from, my local region of Whole Foods. I knew the grocery buyers, the demo coordinators, the receivers, the stockers, and the people in the home office—all the way to the top. Even employees in Kansas, Utah, and New Mexico felt like family to me because I visited those stores, did demos in them, and sent those folks T-shirts and buttons. They even taped coupons to my boxes for me—simply because they knew me. I once asked a grocery team member in Texas to do that. He stumbled around for an answer, then said, "You know, we just can't do that for you. But if you'd like to come in yourself and do it, that would be fine!"

At one point, I had so much money in the business bank account that I could have been ecstatic. I had no debt, and cash was piling up faster than I could imagine. Yet although I felt good about it and there was a sense of relief that I could keep going and have more than enough to pay my bills, seeing those numbers didn't make me feel *happy*. Pleased, yes. Proud of my accomplishments, yes. Stoked that I was making a living selling granola, yes. Relieved that I'd found a way to provide for myself and my daughter while being my own boss, yes. But *happiness* came not in seeing the numbers on my balance sheet but from the contentment I felt that I could make my own schedule and go about my life in a way that seemed good to me. The investment offers also didn't make me feel any happier. What did was being creative, maintaining control of my company, having a flexible schedule, and establishing personal relationships. A whole lot of money wasn't necessary to have those things. And in fact, a whole lot of money may have taken them away from me.

*   *   *

A recurring theme during my walks was the Power of Intention—
Wayne Dyer's idea of a universal energy that lets the act of creation
take place. I had been experimenting with the concept and enjoyed
seeing the results. For some time, I had set the intention of seeing a
bear while out hiking. I can't explain why, but I fancied such an encounter. I had grown up with bears when my family lived on a mountaintop in the middle of a national forest. I missed seeing not only
bears but also the other animals we frequently encountered.

One day on a hike, it happened. I heard a roar but thought it was
a very large dog letting out a cry. I continued on the path until suddenly, I stopped dead in my tracks. The black bear was only twenty
feet away; our eyes made contact. I backed up slowly but held my
gaze. After I'd retreated a few steps, the bear vigorously shook its head,
released another loud roar, and took off through the forest—in the opposite direction. My heart was pounding so loudly I could hear it.
Slowly it regained its rhythm, as did my breathing. I let out a sigh and
smiled. "Wow," I thought, "it happened! I saw a bear, just like I wanted
to!" That incident reaffirmed my belief in the power of visualization
and setting our intentions.

There were other instances. During the last couple of years before
I met Jon, I occasionally walked by the National Center for Atmospheric Research, where he worked, on my way to a hiking trail. "My
next husband works here," I periodically said to myself. "He's probably
in his office right now, doing research. Someday, we will meet." Having
spent my childhood at a solar observatory, I had always felt comfortable around scientists; I enjoyed their quirky senses of humor and
bright minds. One day, after hiking, I went home and drew a picture
of what I thought my next husband would look like. I described his
attributes. I drew a daughter by his side as a friend for Natalie and set
the intention that she would be younger. In the drawing, both he and
his daughter were smiling. Two years after transferring that intention
to paper and tucking it safely away, the four of us met on the bus to
the airport. Every aspect I had described came to fruition.

When I left the company, I started using a new email address with
the name "quetzal," a little bird sacred to both the Aztecs and the

Maya. To protect itself, it stays hidden in the rainforest. After adopting that new identity, my life indeed became solitary as I spent most of my time alone, hidden away, busy with my projects. When I was ready to be visible again, I changed my email address to include the word "gypsy." I set my sights on world travel, meeting new people, and unleashing the free spirit I had tamed to write my book.

I also joined a Nia dance class. Before each session, the instructor gave us a concept to focus on. One day, the focus was inspiration. As we danced, we were to think about what inspires us. I pondered my sources of inspiration: being a mother, nature lover, writer, dancer, Spanish speaker, product developer, cook, traveler, entrepreneur. I felt immense gratitude that most of my adult life had been spent doing things that inspire me. As I danced, I wondered how many people take the time to think about what inspires them.

In the fall of 2014, my mom invited me to Mexico with the group of women I had presented my talk to the year before. One purpose of the trip was to celebrate my fiftieth birthday, and the other was to observe Día de los Muertos in Ajijic, a small artists' community. Young kids from every walk of life in that colorful town are offered free art classes after school and on weekends. They are encouraged to nurture their artistic talents, just for the sake of creating art. There are no strings attached and no expectations. Art is celebrated for the creative endeavor it is, and honored as an integral part of life. The week there was a tribute to the awareness I had gained over the years with my granola company: Being creative is fundamental to leading a balanced life, and its importance should be celebrated. I relished that week, surrounded by art and artists, dynamic women, decorated cemeteries, festive altars, and *catrinas*—those extravagantly dressed skeletons expressing Mexicans' view of death—and the exuberance for life that is ever-present in the local villages.

When I returned home, I decided to continue the festivities. I went to the basement and found the Day of the Dead altar Natalie had made in elementary school. She had decorated a sugar skull and added other adornments: fruit, vegetables, feathers, animals, squares of colored paper, leaves, buttons, flowers, and clay figures. I augmented the altar with photos of our family, offerings to our ancestors, and a few mementos. To welcome and guide our ancestor spirits on their visit, I lit candles and burned incense. Natalie and I had a lovely celebration.

*   *   *

After realizing how effectively the Power of Intention had manifested itself in my life to make Fiona's Granola possible, I continued to explore this intriguing concept. If I could keep a tight grasp on my company despite the many investment offers, conjure up a husband who met my exact specifications, and encounter a bear on the very trail I'd imagined, what else could I achieve? The answer is simple: virtually anything. Each of us has more power to manifest what we desire for our lives than most of us realize. The Law of Attraction states that our focus brings the events we want to fruition.

I decided to have fun with the realization and put the law to its next test. Once I had decided to move to Santa Fe, I visualized the house I wanted to find. I was clear about which rooms would face south and which would face north. I chose the part of town that most appealed to me, my price range, and the proximity to my parents' house. I chose the square footage, number of bedrooms and bathrooms, features I desired, and yard size. I set those specifications and kept my mind focused on them.

During Natalie's spring break, we spent the time house hunting in Santa Fe. We walked through twenty-five homes in five days. One of them met my specifications to a T. Every feature, attribute, and characteristic I had envisioned came to life in that house. Just as amazing, it was available. Homes in that part of town were selling quickly, and the fact that no one had snapped it up seemed incredible. Then I remembered the Power of Intention and the Law of Attraction. Of course the house hadn't sold! The Universe was holding it just for me, because I had focused so keenly on finding it.

I had tried occasionally to share my belief in the Power of Intention with Natalie, and to point out incidents of intentions becoming reality. She didn't seem impressed. But the seed had been planted. I told her that her dreams can also become reality, no matter how elusive they may appear.

After Natalie graduated from high school, my mom invited her on a trip—to anywhere she chose—to acknowledge her academic achievements. Then my mother invited my sister and me along too. Natalie chose a trip to Europe, visiting England, Belgium, France, Germany, and Switzerland.

"Wouldn't it be great," I said to Natalie, "to run into Pito and Eric? It would be so fun to see them!" They had lived across the street from us in Boulder and were our favorite neighbors. They and their two children had moved to Munich for Pito's job four years earlier. Natalie just looked at me, as teen-agers do: "Mom, what are the chances of that?"

I shrugged and said, "Well, you never know." I realized the possibility was a longshot, but I stayed focused on it. During the months leading up to the trip, every so often, I'd say, "Just think, maybe we'll run into Pito and Eric!" She teased me about it, but I continued to visualize the encounter.

One day in Switzerland, we took a cog railway train from a little village up to a majestic spot in the Alps with views of the valleys below. Natalie and I strolled along a hiking trail through fields bursting with wildflowers, stopping occasionally to take in the views. Back at the little train station, I hopped into a cafe to find something to eat before we left. Natalie stayed outside. As I pondered what to buy, a male voice suddenly called out. "Hi, Fiona!" I turned. It was Eric.

"Oh my gosh!" I exclaimed. "I thought this might happen! I've been saying to Natalie for months, 'Maybe we'll run into Pito and Eric.' And here we are!" They had come down from Munich just for the weekend to camp and hike. Eric pointed outside. "There's Pito, talking to Natalie." It was a fun reunion, and we all marveled at it. Natalie and I fell into step as we made our way back to the cog train. As we looked around to enjoy our last glimpse of the majestic mountains, I asked, "Well, honey, are you a believer now?" She just looked at me and smiled. I smiled too, so happy the encounter had come true.

~22~
FINDING FORGIVENESS

"As you go the way of life, you will see a great chasm.
Jump! It is not as wide as you think."

—Joseph Campbell
(Quote on boxes of Orange Crunch Granola)

Shortly before I left the chamber of commerce, a local businessman came in. I told him I would be starting a granola company. His eyes grew wide and he replied, "Wow! That's pretty bold. I didn't think anyone could make a living selling granola."

We can earn a living from the creation of any product, or the offering of any service, if it meets a consumer demand. And if the demand doesn't exist, we can create it. By demonstrating the value of a product or service, and proving its superiority, we can make and retain loyal customers for life. There were dozens of granolas on the market when mine entered the scene, and Fiona's was by far the highest priced. Yet I managed to get much of the town of Boulder hooked. Flavor and quality were part of the equation. Equally important, my company was local, Boulder is a health-conscious town that goes out of its way to support entrepreneurs, and I created a niche market by offering something of quality not already available.

In hindsight, I realize that owning my company was as much a journey of self-discovery as it was managing a business. Entrepreneurs are continually tested: our drive, energy, motivation, stamina, and commitment. Month after month, year after year, we question whether we have what it takes. Are we willing to make endless sacrifices for the good of the business? Are we excited to get up every morning, knowing we'll put in another twelve hours or more? Are we still as revved up about our product or service as the day the crazy idea hit to do this wild thing? Had I not been having fun, had I not had poetic license and unrestricted freedom to create, the sacrifices would not have been worth it.

"Work" for an entrepreneur becomes a lifestyle, and a state of mind. Growing my company—for the most part—was so enjoyable and challenging it didn't seem like work. Running the business was a true salve for the pain of seeing my daughter only half the time. Fiona's Granola became a second child, a tangible entity that energized me and offered another reason to get up in the morning. Just as with my human child, my subsequent creations also required attention, nurturing, love, and commitment. It's not too much of a stretch to compare raising children with growing a company. The same sorts of sacrifices, responsibilities, dedication, and devotion are essential with both.

By maintaining control of my company, my time was spent in fulfilling, personal, and productive ways. By filling my life with so much activity, the days without Natalie passed quickly. The stretches of time without her were emotionally painful, a pain that never subsided. But with my business keeping me over-the-top busy, the time flew by, and suddenly she was back in my arms again. I don't think I could have survived it any other way. My life was full and rich. I was my own boss and the creator of my own destiny. And it stayed that way until I was good and ready to sell my company.

Yes, I made mistakes—plenty of them. The company almost had to shut its doors, and I narrowly escaped bankruptcy. I was close to losing my condo and even closer to losing my mind—a few times. In choosing *not* to give up certain freedoms and decision-making power, I risked more than I should have, and more than most people would have. When people ask if I would do things differently, given the chance, the answer is a resounding, "Yes!" But the core decisions— not to pass off control, not to give up my flexible lifestyle, and not to let anyone limit my creativity—would not change.

The setbacks were learning experiences. It's as if I needed to stumble through the mistakes and learn the lessons, simply by making them and seeing the results. Somehow, I managed to survive, which made getting to the other side all the more satisfying. Through it all, I inspired up-and-coming entrepreneurs, employed dozens of people, and gained recognition for my efforts. I also established a solid company with unlimited potential.

As the Tao dictates, where there is gain, there is also loss. With the sale of the business, the heavy responsibility of owning and managing a company was lifted from my shoulders. But sadness also came, from the new owners' changes to the company. First was the logo: my beloved lotus flowers were replaced by a mountain motif. The boxes became standup pouch bags, with different colors. Most of the text was cut and the rest condensed. The original spirit and character of the packaging was replaced. Customers no longer learn about the ingredients' health benefits, and gone are the inspirational quotes, recipes, and suggestions on ways to enjoy the cereals. Eventually, the granola recipe was changed too, adding pea protein and lentil flour, and replacing the sweetener and oil. The muesli was converted to oatmeal, and sunflower seeds were added to three of the cereals. The company discontinued the Quinoa Crunch, the roasted nuts, the granola bars, and the quinoa bars. It reformulated the trail mixes to include peanuts and sunflower seeds.

The rebranding was a bitter pill. When I opened the case of cereal and trail mix Jarrett sent with the new packaging, my heart sank. The bags no longer characterized the company I had created. I swallowed hard, knowing there was nothing I could do about it.

Separating myself from the business was bittersweet. I had to silence uneasiness and frustration with the new decisions. Friends told me I needed to learn detachment. It was sound advice. When I thought about it, I was reminded of an important aspect of the lotus flower's symbolism: detachment. How perfect: Something I lost—the lotus flowers—represented exactly what I needed to do—detach. It was time to let go.

Even with changes that didn't appeal to me, my relationship with the new owners stayed positive. During the first few months after I left, I continued to provide information and answer questions as needed. I also developed three new granolas that Jarrett wanted for Central Market, a Texas-based grocery chain where the entire Fiona's line was selling well. Its request for additional products was flattering, and I enjoyed participating in the product development.

*   *   *

I had involved Natalie in my professional life both because I had no choice and because she enjoyed it. We both benefitted from the experiences, and I will always feel grateful for them. Admittedly, much of my parenting was unconventional and spontaneous, with few boundaries. Most parents don't rely on their children as confidants and sounding boards the way I depended on my daughter. Sometimes I feel guilty that her childhood lacked the carefree environment many of her friends enjoyed. Then I see how happy and well-rounded she is, and I realize that along with the hardships, there were also many positive experiences. Occasionally, I think how differently our lives could have turned out. But I don't ponder that for long. I look at Natalie and am flooded with wonderful memories of her growing-up years. They sustain me, and most of them I wouldn't trade for the world.

In Natalie's formative years, her horizons were expanded in many ways. Her childhood encouraged the cultivation of her artistic talents, and her creativity added much to the character of my company. The varied experiences and personalities she was exposed to, and her interaction with diverse groups of people, helped shape her into the person she is today. She has grown into a remarkable young lady, bursting with confidence and charisma, and wise beyond her years. As a young adult, her talents continue to find a culinary outlet. One of her favorite hobbies is to cook, bake, and develop healthy treats. I'm glad she enjoys this creative endeavor—and delighted that we share our culinary inspirations.

Life circumstances led me, out of sheer emotional necessity, to use my culinary talents to provide a living for myself and my daughter. Later, people encouraged me to tell my story. I hope it will inspire others—to go for their dreams, jump off that cliff, and trust there is a net that will open. The brave souls who take that leap of faith have a chance to spring higher than they can possibly imagine.

Someone once said, "The only failure is to not have tried." This is true, for how can we succeed if we don't try? A quote hangs in my office: "It's never too late to become who we are meant to be." I believe this to be true, regardless of our age.

I have often thought about the definition of success. My conclusion: it is infinite. We all have different goals and ideas of achievement. For me, success meant bringing joy to people in the form of food and in doing so, touching peoples' lives in a positive way. It meant keeping my business personable, approachable, and fun. I floundered, wavered, and let myself get derailed, more than once. But somehow, I managed to stay the course I had originally set. And that trajectory—staying true to myself, my values, and my goals—ultimately led me to a place of peace at the end of a long and adventurous journey.

I learned valuable lessons from my business. Trust needs to be earned. Goodwill is only as good as its outcome. Dollar signs can blur one's vision. Courage and resilience are options we choose. Others do not have the right to dissuade us from pursuing our dreams. We make mistakes because we have something to learn. Adversity makes us stronger. They are all good lessons, and ones I am extremely grateful to have learned.

As for my dad, only in hindsight do I understand his disapproval of my granola company idea. I interpreted his cool response and initial detachment as lack of confidence in my ability to pull it off. I interpreted his advice to forget the "granola project" as his way of saying he didn't believe in me. His reticence caused me to feel hurt and rejected. He didn't want to be part of a venture he deemed impractical, irresponsible, and risky. He may also have been concerned that not only his daughter but also his granddaughter would find themselves in a financial bind. He was understandably worried about us, and that worry was sincere. It was not bitter or spiteful. Instead, it came from the heart. When he realized I was not to be deterred, he chose to support me the best he could, and he contributed to the growth of the company in the ways he knew how.

I learned about forgiveness. Forgiveness frees the heart. About a year after selling the business, I saw the movie *Invictus*. It made a huge impact on my psyche. Nelson Mandela spent twenty-seven years in prison, and upon his release, immediately forgave those who had imprisoned him. He was behind bars because he had involved himself with human rights, equality, fairness, justice, and respect for all South Africans. He was a pacifist, and his demonstrations were peaceful, yet his government declared him a criminal.

I decided that if I could truly forgive everyone who had hurt me, I would have a lighter heart with which to move forward. I found quotes that helped:

"Forgiveness is a funny thing. It warms the heart and cools the sting."

"Forgiveness does not change the past, but it does enlarge the future."

"To forgive is to set a prisoner free and discover the prisoner was you."

"Forgiveness is not something we do for others. It is something we do for ourselves."

In a quiet ceremony, I forgave those who had caused me mental, emotional, or financial pain. I realized that I hadn't always been easy to work with. Sometimes, my mind had been closed to good ideas. Other times, I hadn't shown my appreciation for the efforts others made on my behalf. I wished I could go back to change those things.

In addition to forgiving others, I realized it was necessary to forgive myself. I had made plenty of mistakes, and if I thought about them too much, depression and anger set in for not doing better. I realized my stubbornness had held me back at times, and that I got in my own way. I found self-forgiveness to be much harder than forgiving others. I kept in mind that I did the best I could. Forgiveness, for myself and others, opened me up like a vessel. It cleared my heart and allowed me to move forward.

The question remains: Would I do it all over again? And the answer is clear: "Yes! Of course I would." How could I not? The passion I feel for my callings—as a writer, traveler, entrepreneur, dancer, Spanish-speaker, and foodie—will propel me to my next adventure. If we don't feed our creativity and nourish the elements that make us who we are, what is our purpose in life? If we have talents and insights we choose not to share, are we worthy enough to possess them? Our duty is to share our gifts— it's why we've been given them. Through sharing, the gift comes alive.

The voice I heard might not be audible for everyone, as was mine. It could instead be a persistent feeling or a daydream or a vision of doing something differently. In whatever form it makes its presence known, it is to be honored. Perhaps the message lies in the passion and happiness we feel doing a certain thing, and that certain thing brings joy each time we do it. Whatever creative endeavor brings us joy, I believe, is Divine presence.

*   *   *

I moved to New Mexico after Natalie graduated from high school. My decision was not easy, as it would mean less time together. But she was off to Denver, and there would only be a six-hour drive between us. I had fallen in love with Santa Fe and felt at home in northern New Mexico. Jon also relocated to Santa Fe, and our friendship continued.

In Santa Fe from time to time, I see people I knew in Boulder, most of them farmers market customers or Whole Foods employees. They seem happy to see me. One woman said, "Oh, Fiona! I just ate your granola for breakfast this morning!" It's fun to know I've left a legacy, and it has warmed my heart to hear people say they've missed me.

*   *   *

I am thankful for this book. Through writing it, I acquired a new appreciation for the unique and very special relationship I share with my daughter. The gratitude I feel toward my parents, who offered support despite their doubts, was also renewed. I am thankful also for the personal relationships that grew out of, and were nurtured by, the business I began. I am grateful for the many life lessons learned along the way. I feel endless gratitude that I honored my creativity—and still do, and always will. Living on the edge and going against convention can be daunting. Nonconformity means allowing the unknown to lead us. The next adventure, until it unfolds, is a mystery. By living life this way, from creative endeavor to creative endeavor, our very future is a mystery. The path has yet to reveal itself. Which creative flow will take us to that place our spirits long to go? Which inspiration will we follow? These are the questions that beckon, the ones that will be answered. It takes only finding that place of trust, and belief in ourselves, to let our dreams be fulfilled. When we no longer hold back from that which beckons us forward, which lights our fire, which makes us feel alive, we can truly start living. Our passions should not be ignored; they should be ignited.

May we all be alive. And may we all follow our hearts, discover our passions, and seek our next adventures.

A Sincere Thank You

I extend thanks to many people:

- My beloved daughter, Natalie, whose patience, humor, open-mindedness, goodwill, and imagination added much delight to our adventure.
- My parents, who jumped on the granola bandwagon and supported my efforts.
- Grocery buyers and customers who supported my endeavors.
- My "family and friends" editors: my daughter Natalie, my mother Patricia, and my friend Suzanne.
- My professional editor: Marty Gerber. Your suggestions greatly improved the readability of the text.
- My publisher: Terra Nova Books. Your belief in this book allowed the narrative, and its message, to be shared.
- And many thanks to all those who encouraged me to share my story.

About the Author

Fiona Maria Simon was born and raised in a tiny mountaintop community in southern New Mexico. Former owner of Fiona's Natural Foods, she holds a bachelor's degree in history and a master's in Spanish and Latin American literature. She has worked as an editor, travel writer, journalist, and language instructor. An avid traveler, dancer, and outdoor enthusiast, she also loves to cook, bake, and develop healthy food products. Her hobbies include hiking, biking, and exploring other cultures. Simon enjoys live music, expanding her cultural horizons, spiritual growth, and inspiring and empowering others with her story.